DISCO

C000043411

1 Find a time when you can read the Bible each day

2 Find a place where you can be quiet and think

4 Ask God to help you understand what you read

3 Grab your Bible and a pencil or pen

5 Read today's Discover page and Bible bit

6 Pray about what you have read and learned

We want to...
- Explain the Bible clearly to you
- Help you enjoy your Bible
- Encourage you to turn to Jesus
- Help Christians follow Jesus

Discover stands for...
- Total commitment to God's Word, the Bible
- Total commitment to getting its message over to you

Team Discover

Martin Cole, Nicole Carter, Rachel Jones, Kirsty McAllister, Alison Mitchell, André Parker, Ben Woodcraft
Discover is published by The Good Book Company, Blenheim House, 1 Blenheim Rd, Epsom, Surrey, KT19 9AP, UK.
Tel: 0333 123 0880; Email: discover@thegoodbook.co.uk UK: thegoodbook.co.uk
North America: thegoodbook.com Australia: thegoodbook.com.au NZ: thegoodbook.co.nz

How to use Discover

Here at Discover, we want you at home to get the most out of reading the Bible. It's how God speaks to us today. And He's got loads of top things to say.

We use the New International Version (NIV) of the Bible. You'll find that the NIV and New King James Version are best for doing the puzzles in Discover.

The Bible has 66 different books in it. So if the notes say...

Read James 3 v 1

...turn to the contents page of your Bible and look down the list of books to see what page James begins on. Turn to that page.

"James 3 v 1" means you need to go to chapter 3 of James, and then find verse 1 of chapter 3 (the verse numbers are the tiny ones). Then jump in and read it!

Here's some other stuff you might come across...

WEIRD WORDS

Trimplegraw
These boxes explain baffling words or phrases we come across in the Bible.

Think!

This bit usually has a tricky personal question on what you've been reading about.

Action!

Challenges you to put what you've read into action.

Wow!

This section contains a gobsmacking fact that sums up what you've been reading about.

Pray!

Gives you ideas for prayer. Prayer is talking to God. Don't be embarrassed! You can pray in your head if you want to. God still hears you! Even if there isn't a Pray! symbol, it's a good idea to pray about what you've read anyway.

Coming up in Issue 7...

James: Fantastic faith

Ever blurted something out and then instantly wished you hadn't?

Yup, me too.

The book of James has loads of great advice for keeping control of our tongues. James wrote his letter to Jewish Christians just a few decades after Jesus returned to heaven. James says that when Jesus changes you on the inside, that should change everything you say (and do) too. And James isn't afraid to use some strong words to get his point across! From conflict to complaining, this is one you definitely don't want to miss.

Exodus: God rules, OK?

We join the Israelites in the desert for the final instalment of Exodus. But this is no fun camping trip (although there is a *very* special tent involved…).

God has rescued the Israelites from slavery in Egypt, looked after them on their journey, and is leading them to a brilliant new home in the promised land. Now God gives them rules to help them live the best way — HIS way.

Trouble is, the Israelites are TERRIBLE at keeping them! And we're just the same. So Exodus is a great reminder of how much we need God's forgiveness too.

Revelation: Jesus revealed

It's pretty easy to find the book of Revelation in your Bible — because it's right at the very end!

Revelation means revealing something. God gave John (one of the twelve disciples) loads of strange visions: we'll read about thrones, lampstands, scrolls, colourful horses, earthquakes, trumpets, angels, beasts, a lamb and a dragon! But really it's all about JESUS!!

Revelation tells us crucial stuff that is going to happen, and also stuff that has happened and is happening now! We'll see that God is in total control, and even get an exciting glimpse of what heaven is like!

John: Unbeatable love

If you knew you only had 24 hours left to live, what would you do with them? Only the things that were really important to you, right?

Jesus used the night before he died to do a *lot* of talking — and this stuff is *super* important. Jesus wanted to tell his disciples why he needed to die, and reassure them about what would happen after he was gone. One of his disciples, John, wrote it all down so that we can listen in too!

Turn the page to get started...

James: Fantastic faith

James
3 v 1-6

rudder

2000 years ago James wrote a letter to Christians, telling them how they could live for God in an ungodly world.

It's great for Christians today too. We started reading James in the last issue of Discover. So let's pick it up halfway through...

WEIRD WORDS

Stumble
Mess up and let God down

Corrupts
Messes up

In check
Under control

Ridiculous riddle

We all have one.

It's quite small but affects the whole of our lives.

It helps us to make people smile or upset them.

What is it?

Taungc

Read James 3 v 1-5

What's the answer?

TO

I'll accept mouth as a right answer too. James says that the tongue is like a ship's rudder.

It's very small but controls a large and important thing — us.

Think!

Have you got your tongue under control?

Or do you say...

| the first thing that comes into your head? | hurtful things about people? | things that you know are wrong? |

Read verse 6

What else is the tongue like?

Judgements a

Just like fire, our words can cause lots of damage. They can hurt people, mess up friendships and have a huge effect on our lives. James says that the devil tempts us to say wrong things. So we need God's help to use our tongues in the right way!

Think again!

What bad things have you said recently?

snapping at
Mum

Pray!

Say sorry to God for those things. Ask God to help you think before you speak. Ask him to help you to say things that please Him.

Tongue-taming time

James 3 v 7-12

James is telling us how dangerous our tongues can be.

What we say is so important.

WEIRD WORDS

Curse
Say bad things about someone

Made in God's likeness
Humans show something of what God is like!

Salt spring
Salty water springing from underground

Read James 3 v 7-8

Do you think you could tame a vicious snake or wild animal if you suddenly met one?

YES/NO _____

Probably not! James says it's even harder to tame our tongues. We try not to offend our parents, but we just lose control and let it out. Or we decide to stop swearing, but when we're with our friends, we just can't help it.

Think!

But God can help us tame our tongues! In what ways do you mess up with your words?

_____

_____

_____

Pray!

Now ask God to help you tame your tongue so you stop doing those things. It could take a long time, so keep asking!

Read James 3 v 9-12

Some people say they're Christians yet they often swear, tell dirty jokes, or say unkind things to people.

If you're a Christian, should you be saying these things?

YES/NO _____

> **A fresh-water spring always gives fresh water**

> **A fig tree always produces figs, not other fruit**

> **So a Christian should always say _____ things**

Wow!

But Christians do still mess up and say stuff we shouldn't. When we do, we need to say sorry to God and ask Him to help us sort it out.

Think & pray!

What about you? What sort of things do you say? Maybe you want to pray again for God to change you inside and help you say good things that are pleasing to Him.

**James
3 v 13-18**

Wise words

O	C	P	D	W	V	A	U	F	N
E	O	G	S	I	N	C	E	R	E
F	N	E	T	X	P	D	N	G	N
R	S	H	C	Y	U	X	T	O	V
B	I	T	T	E	R	D	S	E	Y
M	D	Q	A	L	E	F	E	K	A
P	E	A	C	E	F	U	L	M	H
U	R	S	N	J	Z	K	F	G	Q
R	A	S	K	C	J	Y	I	L	B
L	T	B	B	V	I	C	S	H	Z
J	E	A	L	O	U	S	H	P	J

Do you think you're wise?

YES/NO _____

Read James 3 v 13

James says if you're really wise, you'll show it by serving God, doing good deeds and putting others first. James says there are two kinds of wisdom: **earthly** wisdom (fake) and **godly** wisdom.

Read verses 14-16

Find words in the wordsearch to show what earthly wisdom is like.

Earthly wisdom

J_____

B_____

S_____

E_____

WEIRD WORDS

Humility
Putting other people first

Harbour bitter envy
Stay jealous

Selfish ambition
Putting yourself first

Unspiritual
Not godly

Disorder
Chaos, mess

Submissive
Obeying God

Mercy
Forgiveness

Good fruit
Good deeds

Impartial
Fair

Sincere
Not fake

Righteousness
Godliness

Earthly wisdom
**Putting yourself first
Having bitter thoughts
Getting jealous of people**

These things happen all the time. But this is earthly wisdom and comes from the devil (v15). We should try to cut these things out.

Read verses 17-18

Godly wisdom

P_____

P_____

C_____

S_____

Godly wisdom
**Putting others first
Forgiving people
Peacefully sorting things out
Doing good deeds**

These things are **truly wise**. Real wisdom comes from heaven (v17). God gives it to us — so we can ask Him for it!

Pray!

Ask God to make you wise. Ask Him to help you be less selfish, more pure, loving, forgiving and considerate.

4

James 4 v 1-6

Fighting talk today from James.

Sort it out!

Read the verses and fill in the spaces to reveal what James is teaching us today.

Read James 4 v 1

Your quarrels and fights come from your _____

_____

_____

Do you argue with friends because you're selfishly putting yourself first?

Read verse 2

When you want something, you fight and covet. You don't get it because _____

_____

_____

Do you argue when you don't get your own way?

Do you long for stuff that other people have?

Do you ask God for the things you need?

Read verse 3

When you ask God, you don't receive because you ask with _____

_____

We shouldn't ask God for nice stuff we selfishly want, like a new bike. We should ask Him for things that **please Him**, like becoming more loving.

If you really **need** a new bike, ask God for one, but don't get selfish and greedy.

Read verse 4

Anyone who is a friend of the world becomes

_____

We have to choose between living the world's selfish, sinful way, or living God's way.

Read verses 5-6

God shows _____
to the _____

It's really hard to be unselfish and live God's way. But God lovingly helps us turn away from sin and serve Him more.

Pray!

Ask God to help you put others first, not argue so much, and not long for stuff you don't have. Ask Him to help you turn your back on your selfish ways so that you really live for Him!

WEIRD WORDS

Covet
Wanting someone else's stuff

Wrong motives
Selfish reasons

Adulterous
They claimed to be God's people but loved the world and lived for themselves

Scripture
Old Testament

Enmity
Being at war

Grace
God gives us far more than we deserve

5

Clean your heart

James
4 v 7-10

Look back at yesterday's Discover page.

If you're like me, you'll be feeling bad for putting yourself first instead of God.

But James knows exactly what we need to do...

Read James v 7-10

Pretty tricky to understand, eh? Use the words down the centre to fill in the gaps. Then read the explanation below.

S_____ yourselves to God (v7). Change your l_____ into c_____ (v9). H_____ yourselves before the L_____ and he will l_____ you up (v10).

1. ADMIT to God that you've done wrong.

Tell Him how sorry you are and how bad you feel for letting Him down.

R_____ the d_____ and he will flee from y_____ (v7).

2. DON'T GIVE IN to the devil's temptations. Fight against doing wrong. Keep living God's way and the devil will one day give up on you. In the end, God will win and the devil will lose!

Come n_____ to G____ and He will c_____ near to you (v8).

come crying devil God hands hearts Humble laughter lift Lord near purify Resist Submit Wash you

3. COME NEAR TO GOD. Just going to church and appearing to be a Christian isn't enough. We've got to actively try to live God's way. We've got to obey Him, spend more time talking to Him and reading the Bible!

W_____ your h_____ and p_____ your h_____ (v8).

4. TURN AWAY from the wrong stuff you do and turn to Jesus. He died to make sinful people clean. We wash our **hearts** when we trust in Jesus and live for Him.

Pray!

It's all tough stuff to do. We need God's help. Read through the explanations again and ask God to help you do those things. Then do them!

Don't judge or grudge

James
4 v 11-12

Are you sitting comfortably?

Well you won't be for long because I want you to answer an uncomfortable question...

WEIRD WORDS

Slander
Say untrue things about someone

The law
The way God wants us to live

What nasty things have you said about people recently?

_____

_____

_____

_____

Tom and Josh are having a play fight, but Tom gets hurt and goes off to sulk. Emma, who likes to get involved in things, spots Tom and goes over to him...

Who's upset you, Tom?

It was Josh, but...

interrupting What an idiot! I'll sort him out!

So Emma tells her friends how nasty Josh is and they ignore him and give him a hard time.

Read James 4 v 11

In our story, who was slandering someone else?

Who was setting themselves up as a judge?

Of course the answer is Emma. She was so busy thinking how wrong Josh had been, yet she was the one most at fault.

Think!

Do YOU ever say nasty things about other people? Things that you would hate to be said about you?

YES/NO _____

Read verse 12

Who has given laws to say what is right and wrong? And who will judge everyone at the end of the world?

Only God decides what is right and wrong. Only God is perfect. Only God can judge people. So we've got to stop judging others!

Pray!

Say sorry to God for the times you've slandered and judged others. Ask Him to help you say positive things about people, and not negative stuff.

1

**James
4 v 13-17**

What are some of the things you plan to do before the end of the year?

_____
_____
_____
_____
_____
_____
_____
_____
_____
_____
_____
_____

Mist opportunity

Read James 4 v 13-14

Don't worry, James isn't saying it's wrong to make exciting plans! He's talking about people who **ignore God** in their plans.

What does James say we're like? (v14)

[ ]

Wow!

Mist or smoke doesn't last for long. And, compared to God, we're not around on earth for very long. But God has always existed and will always exist. He's in control. We're not. So we should look to God when we're making plans.

Before   **After**

Read verses 15-16

Decide whether each sentence is the right or wrong attitude to making plans. Circle the letters in the correct column.

	Right	Wrong
Pray about your plans	HU	TRE
Do things without thinking	RN	BOA
Do what pleases you	AT	STF
Ask if it's God's will	MB	AN
Be ready to change your plans for God	LE	ED
Do things your own way	OND	UL

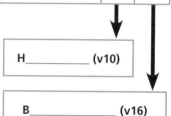

H_____ (v10)

B_____ (v16)

Which of those two words is most like you?

[ ]

Read verse 17

It's not just doing the wrong thing that's sinful. If you don't do the right thing, that's just as bad.

Pray!

Tell God about your plans. Ask Him to show you if they're ok or not. And ask Him to help you do things to serve Him. (Grab some spare paper, and jot down ways you can serve God this week.)

Common wealth gains

**James
5 v 1-6**

*James is really
furious!*

WEIRD WORDS

Corroded
Worn out

Testify
Give evidence

Hoarded
Selfishly stored up

Harvesters
People who gather
the crops

Self indulgence
Spending all your
money on yourself

Condemned
Sentenced to death

Opposing
Against

Read James 5 v 1-3

These people are loaded.

*But what does James say has
happened to their money?*

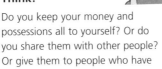

Your wealth has

r_____ (v2)

These people cared too much about
money. But James says their money
might as well be rotting, because
they haven't used it to serve God
(like giving to the church or to the
poor).

Think!

Do you keep your money and
possessions all to yourself? Or do
you share them with other people?
Or give them to people who have
very little?

Read verses 4-6

These people did anything they
could to make more money.
Including treating others really
badly. *What should they have done
with their money? Tick two.*

| Paid the wages they owed |
| Put it all in the bank |
| Bought an ostrich farm |
| Given it to poor people |

These people were living to
make money and to please only
themselves. They didn't care about
God or about other people. One
day, God will punish anyone who
lives for themselves and not for Him.

Action!

How can you serve God with your
money and possessions? What can
you share or give away or give to
charity?

_____

_____

_____

Pray!

Ask God to help you be more
unselfish with your money and
possessions, and to do the things
you've written down.

9

**James
5 v 7-11**

Mustn't grumble

Yesterday, James came down hard on selfish, rich people. Today he tells Christians how to deal with those people and how to cope with tough times.

Read James 5 v 7-11

What does James say we should do (v7)? Unjumble the anagrams.

Be p_____

       e a t p i n t

Life is not perfect, and at times it seems unfair, but James says be patient!

Be patient like a

f_____

   r a m r e f

He plants seeds, then has to wait for months and months before they grow into crops that he can eat and sell.

These guys might be poor and badly treated but they should stick with it and wait for the…

L_____ c_____

 s o L d r   m i g c o n

When Jesus comes again, they will go to live for ever with Him. That's far better than any amount of money!

James mentions how Job had a really tough time (v11). Yet he didn't turn away from the Lord, and he will live with God for ever! God is so loving and kind to those who stick with Him through tough times. He gives Christians the strength to keep going, and one day they'll be rewarded with eternal life.

Read verse 9 again

Don't g_____

       b l u r g e m

Don't moan that other people have more than you, or blame God when life seems hard.

Wow!

What have you been grumbling about recently?

_____

_____

_____

_____

_____

_____

Pray!

Tell God about your complaints and ask Him to sort them out. Ask Him to help you be patient until He returns, when Christians will go to live with Him for ever!

WEIRD WORDS

Yield
Give/produce

The Judge
Jesus, who will one day return to judge everyone who has rejected Him

Prophets
God's messengers

Blessed
Privileged to serve God

Persevered
Kept living God's way

Job
Godly man who suffered loads

Compassion
Loving kindness

Swear box

James
5 v 12

Write down some promises you've not been able to keep.

_____

_____

_____

_____

I promise I'll feed the cat every day

Ever made a promise you wish you hadn't?

You want to keep it, but it's sooo hard.

In Bible times, people would make a promise

I'll feed your camel every day

with a vow added:

I swear it in God's name

The Pharisees argued that if your promise didn't mention God, then you didn't have to keep it. Crazy! This was twisting God's law and it led to lots of crafty lying.

James said these promises were wrong because God's name and things to do with God were being used in a disrespectful way.

Read James 5 v 12

Think!

Do you use God's name carelessly? Maybe you say "Oh my God!" without even realising it.

James says don't make promises carelessly or say unnecessary things (like "I swear on my gran's deathbed"). *Crack the code to reveal James' advice.*

All you need to say is…

Action!

Try to be honest. Mean what you say, and say what you mean. And if you do make a promise, try to keep it!
Ask God to help you be honest with people and keep your promises.

WEIRD WORDS

Swear
Make a promise

Condemned
Punished by God

A	B	C	D	E	F	G	H	I	K	L	M	N	O	P	R	S	T	U	W	Y

If in doubt, pray!

**James
5 v 13-18**

*Are you happy
or sad at the
moment?*

_____

WEIRD WORDS

Elders
Church leaders

**Anoint them
with oil**
Pour oil on their
head. I'm not really
sure why!

Righteous person
Someone who lives
God's way

Elijah
Prophet in the Old
Testament. God used
him to do amazing
things!

Earnestly
Seriously

What do you do to help you cope
when life is tough?

_____

_____

_____

And what do you do to show you're
happy?

_____

_____

Read James 5 v 13

*What should we do when we're in
trouble?*

P_____

What about when we're happy?

Pr_____ God

Action!

If you're finding life hard, the first
thing you should do is PRAY. Ask
God to help. If you're happy, you
should PRAY too! Thank God for
giving you happiness.

Read verses 14-18

**If anyone is s_____ they
should get the church
e_____ to p_____
for them (v14)**

If someone you know is ill, grab
other Christians to pray about it.

Remember, God always answers our
prayers, although not always in the
way we might expect. It's not always
God's plan to heal people instantly.

**Confess your s_____

to each other and p_____

for each other (v16)**

It's a great idea to get together
regularly with other Christians to
pray. You can talk about the sin
you're struggling with and pray
about it.

In verses 17-18 James mentions
how Elijah's prayers were answered
in amazing ways (you can find it in
1 Kings chapters 17 and 18). **God
listens to us! He answers our
prayers!**

Pray!

If you're in trouble, ask God to
help you.
If you're happy, praise Him!
If you're ill, ask God to make you
better.
If you've done wrong, admit it to
God and say sorry.

12

You to the rescue?

James 5 v 19-20

James has been showing us how to live for God in an ungodly world.

He finishes his letter with a few final instructions...

You're standing at the train station waiting for the 10.20 to Rochdale. To your horror, you see a doddery old man wandering dangerously close to the edge as a fast train is approaching.

Do you...

a) **look the other way and hope for the best?** ☐

b) **run to him and guide him away from the edge?** ☐

c) **phone a friend?** ☐

Read James 5 v 19-20

Becky is a friend from church. She says she's a Christian, but recently she's been going off the rails: using bad language, getting into trouble and even saying she's not sure if the Bible is true.

What would you do?

a) **Calmly chat with her, trying to point her back to living God's way** ☐

b) **Pray for her loads** ☐

c) **If she won't listen, ask an older Christian to help** ☐

I hope you ticked all three answers! Often when we see a friend turning away from God, we're too scared to say anything to them. Or we just gossip about them behind their backs.

James says that Christians should look out for one another and help each other to keep living God's way.

Prayer action!

Do you know anyone who has turned away from God?

_____

_____

Ask God to bring them back to living His way. And think how you might be able to lovingly point them back in the right direction.

Well done for finishing James' letter! If you have any questions email them to: discover@thegoodbook.co.uk

13

Time to join the Israelites in the desert in the book of Exodus.

Exodus: God rules, OK?

The story so far...

• God has rescued Moses and the Israelites from slavery in Egypt

• They've been travelling in the desert for 3 months, with God looking after them

• Now it's time for them to STOP and LISTEN to God

Read Exodus 19 v 1-4

It's easy to wander through life without thinking much about God. We need to **STOP** and **LISTEN** to God. That's what we're doing when we read the Bible. That's how God speaks to us.

Just a few months earlier, God's people had been slaves in Egypt.

Who had rescued them?

God had brought them out of Egypt, helped them to cross the Red Sea, and killed their enemies, the Egyptians. Like an eagle cares for her young, God had powerfully rescued them from danger and brought them to live with Him (v4).

Read verses 5-6

Fill in the missing vowels (aeiou) to reveal God's great promise to the Israelites.

If you ob__y me f__lly and k__ __p my c__v__n__nt, you will be my chosen p__ __pl__, my tr__ __sured p__ss__ssion. You will be a k__ngd__m of pr__ __sts, serving me.

Wow!

God had done so much for the Israelites, and He promised them more amazing things. God has done so much for us too! He sent His Son Jesus to RESCUE us from sin.

If we are Christians, then:

• He is our rescuing King

• we are His rescued people

• we're privileged to serve Him

Pray!

Thank God for sending Jesus to rescue people. Ask God to help you to serve Him as one of His people.

**Exodus
19 v 7-15**

*How would
you feel about
being chosen
as the Queen
of England's
personal servant?*

_____

_____

_____

WEIRD WORDS

Elders
Leaders

Consecrate
Make them clean
and ready for God

Ram's horn
Sheep's horn used as
a trumpet!

Abstain
Don't do it

Keep it clean

God, the King of the universe, had
chosen the Israelites to serve Him.
But how would the people respond
to this great news?

Find out in Exodus 19 v 7-8

> We will do...
>
> _____
>
> _____ **(v8)**

Think!

Is that YOUR attitude towards
obeying God? Do you try to do
everything He commands in the
Bible?

It's one thing to be **willing** to serve
God, it's another to actually be
ready for the job! God had some
special instructions...

Read verses 9-11

... and fill in the missing words.

1. Be clean!

They had to w_____ their

c_____ (v10)

to get ready for God.

God is perfect. People have to be
clean and ready to meet Him. For us
that means having our sins forgiven.

Read verses 12-15

2. Keep your distance

Moses put limits around the

m_____. No one

was allowed to t_____

the mountain. Anyone who

did was put to d_____

(v12).

God was going to put on a display
of His awesome power. The people
would watch... at a distance. Only
Moses was allowed to go up the
mountain to be with God.

We can't just walk up to God! We
have no right to get anywhere near
God. He's too perfect.

Wow!

But the great news is that...

JESUS washes away sin so we can
come and worship our holy and
perfect God!

JESUS brings believers near to God,
so they no longer need to keep their
distance!

Pray!

Thank God that you can talk to
Him right now because Jesus has
made it possible!

Thunder struck

**Exodus
19 v 16-25**

*The day had
arrived. A day the
Israelites would
remember for the
rest of their lives.*

*They would never
forget the time
God spoke with
Moses.*

Get ready for an amazing scene. Try
to imagine being there.

Read Exodus 19 v 16-19

*You'll find all the answers in the
wordsearch (and the verses).*

They saw

l_ _ _ _ _ _ _ _ _,

f_ _ _ and s_ _ _ _ _

They heard

t_ _ _ _ _ _r and

a t_ _ _ _ _ _t and God's

v_ _ _ _

They felt an

e_ _ _ _ _ _ _ _ke

They were

a_ _ _ _ _ so they

t_ _ _ _ _ _d

E	B	T	R	E	M	B	L	E	D
L	G	N	A	F	V	D	T	A	O
I	J	T	L	Z	F	C	H	R	T
G	A	L	G	C	I	K	U	T	V
H	F	D	J	S	R	O	N	H	U
T	R	U	M	P	E	T	D	Q	R
N	A	R	E	N	K	X	E	U	X
I	I	U	B	H	P	F	R	A	S
N	D	H	A	L	S	M	O	K	E
G	L	B	C	V	O	I	C	E	P

The people saw how powerful God
was! You can imagine how stunned
they must have been!

But God was worried that curiosity
might get the better of them...

Read verses 20-25

Moses had set up barriers around
the mountain. Surely no one would
dare disobey God and come up the
mountain, would they? But God told
Moses to warn them again so no
one would get hurt.

Think!

Do you ever forget how great and
powerful God is? Ever forget that
what you read in the Bible are the
words of this great and holy God?

Pray!

Ask God to help you take His
words seriously. And to remember
who you're talking to when you
pray!

WEIRD WORDS

Descended
Came down

Perish
Die

Consecrate
Clean, purify

Break out
Punish

Holy
Perfect, pure

Top ten commandments

**Exodus
20 v 1-6**

*God is speaking
to Moses on
Mount Sinai,
and He has some
hugely important
things to say.*

*God is going to
tell His people
how they should
live for Him.*

WEIRD WORDS

Jealous
God is determined
that people won't
worship anything or
anyone else but Him

**Third and fourth
generation**
Their grandchildren
and great-
grandchildren.

Read Exodus 20 v 1-2

*What does God remind the Israelites
(v2)?*

> I am the L_____
> your G_____ who
> brought you out of
> E_____, the land of
> s_____.

He is their God. They are His people.
And they need to understand some
ground rules for serving Him.

Read verses 3-6

Do you recognise verses 3 and 4?
They are the first two of the **Ten
Commandments!**

God gave the Israelites lots of
rules to show them how to live in
a way that pleased Him. The Ten
Commandments sum up all of these
rules. They're a good guide for us
too, to help us please God.

10 Commandments
1. No other gods! (v3)
2. No idols! (v4)

In other words, **NOTHING** should
take God's place in our lives.

An **IDOL** is anything we worship
instead of God. In Bible times,
people often made statues to
pray to. But an idol today can be
anything we treat as being more
important than God.

*Have a think about what you might
be tempted to put first instead of
God. The pics in the box might
help you. Draw or write any of your
own...*

Pray!

We all break these two
commandments! None of us
always put God first. Tell God
you're sorry for letting other
things be more important to you
than He is. Ask Him to help you
love Him more than anything else.

Rest is best

**Exodus
20 v 7-11**

*God is giving the
Israelites the Ten
Commandments.*

*Let's check out
numbers 3 and 4.*

WEIRD WORDS

Misuse
Use in a disrespectful
way

Sabbath
The special day when
Israelites rested from
work

Holy
Set apart for God

Labour
Work hard

10 Commandments

3. Don't misuse God's name

4. Keep the Sabbath holy

Read Exodus 20 v 7
So what does that mean exactly?

> **It means don't joke
> about God.**

> **And never use God's
> name (or Jesus) as a
> swear word.**

> **And don't think
> wrong things about
> God.**

God is the Creator of the world.
And even though we've sinned
against Him, He sent Jesus to
take the punishment we deserve.
We should give God soooo much
respect. He deserves it!

Think!

Do you do any of the things in the
speech bubbles? What do you say
when you hear people using God's
name wrongly?

Read verses 8-11
God made our world and then
rested (v11). In the same way, the
Israelites were to work for six days
and then have a day of rest.

But a day of rest doesn't mean
spending all day sleeping!

Fill in the missing vowels (aeiou).

It's a great day to
m_ _t with other
Chr_st_ans, to learn
t_g_ther about J_sus.
It's also a great day to do
s_m_th_ng you _nj_y

Action!

*What will you do to make one day a
week special?*

**Get outside and enjoy the
world God has made?** ☐

**Do something you enjoy and
thank God for it?** ☐

**Help God's people (church)
do God's work?** ☐

Meet up with Christians? ☐

Pray!

Read the Think! and Action!
sections again. Ask God to help
you with these things.

Dadly sin

**Exodus
20 v 12**

When was the
last time you
upset your mum
or dad, and what
did you do?

_____

_____

_____

_____

There are times
when we all
wish the fifth
commandment
had never been
written!

Read Exodus 20 v 12

10 Commandments
5. Honour your parents!

*Do you honour (respect) your
parents or guardians? Look at
the list below and mark yourself
honestly! Write **rarely**, **sometimes**,
or **always** next to each one.*

	rarely/sometimes/always
Obey them	
Be polite to them	
Help them	
Listen to them	
Thank them	

*How do you react when you're
asked to do something?*

a) **complain** ☐

b) **hide** ☐

c) **put it off** ☐

d) **obey straight away** ☐

There's a great reason why we
should always give answer **d**.

Find it by crossing out all the Xs.

XXCHIXLXXDRXXENO

XXXBEYYOXUXRXXPAX

REXNTSXXINXEVERXXX

XYTXHIXNXGXXFOXXRT

HXXIXXSPXLEXXASXES

TXXHEXXLOXXRDXXX

C_____

_____

_____

_____

(Colossians 3 v 20)

Action!

Circle what you'll do...

**Obey them
without grumbling**

Tell them you love them

**Thank them for all
they do for you**

**Help at home
without being asked**

Pray!

Say sorry to God for the times
you've not honoured your
parents. Ask Him to help you to
do the things you've circled.
Now go and do them!

Murder mystery

**Exodus
20 v 13-15**

*Ever murdered
anyone?*

*Or cheated on
your husband?*

*Or broken into a
house?*

Me neither!

*So I guess
commandments
6, 7 and 8 don't
apply to us.
Right?*

WEIRD WORDS

Adultery
Cheating on your
husband or wife

Wrong! They **do** apply to us.

Read Exodus 20 v 13-15

10 Commandments
6. Don't murder
7. Don't commit adultery
8. Don't steal

Jesus makes it clear that these
commandments also include wrong
stuff that most of us do.

Read Matthew 5 v 21-22

Don't murder
*What else is covered by this
commandment (v22)?*

Getting a_____

Calling people n_____

*Done either of these things
recently?*

Yes/No _____

Read Matthew 5 v 27-28

Don't commit adultery
Anyone who looks at a

w_____ lustfully

commits a_____ in

his h_____

We've got to watch out for wrong
thoughts.

Pray!
Do you know anyone whose
family has broken up? Maybe
yours? Pray for that family. Ask
God to help them through tough
times. Pray that they will turn to
Him for help.

Don't steal
Have you ever...

**taken stuff you weren't
supposed to?**

**borrowed something and
not returned it?**

**dodged paying for
something?**

If we do any of these things we
cheat and hurt others — AND GOD!

Pray!
Say sorry to God for specific
times you've messed up with
commandments 6, 7 and 8. Ask
Him to help you cut out these
wrong things.

Look into your lies

**Exodus
20 v 16-17**

God is giving Moses and the Israelites ten special rules to show them how to live their lives for Him. The Ten Commandments.

Let's look at the last two...

WEIRD WORDS

False testimony
Telling lies about someone

Neighbour
Anyone you meet

Covet
Wanting someone else's things

---

10 Commandments
9. Don't lie
10. Don't covet

Read Exodus 20 v 16

> I hate Lauren. Let's tell Mr Harris that she stole some of your stuff.

> Great idea. That will show her who's boss.

Tick the reasons why that's wrong.

God's 9th commandment says it's wrong ☐

Lauren would be punished for something she hadn't done ☐

God's people should only speak the truth, as God does ☐

God's people should love each other, just as God loves them ☐

All of these answers are true. The Ten Commandments showed God's people, the Israelites, how to live. They were to be like Him, and show others what He is like. God is **loving** and **truthful**. They should be too. And so should Christians today!

Read verse 17

Draw a star next to things the Israelites were told not to covet.

You've probably never wanted someone else's ox! But circle the pics of things you might get jealous about.

> God doesn't really love me. He hasn't given me enough. I want more!

You wouldn't say anything like that, would you?! But if you're jealous of what other people have, that **is** what you're saying to God. It's like saying that God hasn't given you enough.

Pray!

Say sorry to God for times you've lied about people. Ask Him to help you tell the truth.
Say sorry for times you've wanted other people's stuff. Ask God to help you be satisfied with what He's given you.

**Exodus
20 v 18-21**

*At the top of the
mountain, God
gave Moses 10
rules to show the
Israelites how to
serve Him.*

*There was lots of
thunder, lightning
and noise.*

*The people were
terrified.*

Scary stuff

Think!

1. Do you love God?

Yes/No _____

2. Are you afraid of God?

Yes/No _____

Now let's find out if you're telling
the truth...

Read Exodus 20 v 18-21

*There were two kinds of fear.
Fill in the gaps to reveal them.*

**When they saw the
th_____ and lightning,
they tr_____d in
f_____ (v18).**

> **1. The people were AFRAID
> of God and what He might
> do to them.**

**Moses said, "Do not be
a_____. God has
come to t_____ you so
that the f_____ of the
Lord will keep you from
s_____." (v20)**

> **2. Moses told them to fear
> God in a different way. To
> show great respect for Him.
> To LOVE and OBEY God.**

What kind of **fear** do the Ten
Commandments give **YOU**?

1. Do they make you AFRAID of God?

- Because you've failed to obey
  them loads of times?

- Because God hates our sin?

- Because God will punish sin with
  hell?

Wow!

But we don't need to be afraid,
because Jesus can forgive our sin. If
you're a Christian, God has already
forgiven you! So you don't need to
be afraid!

2. Do they make you LOVE God and OBEY Him?

- Because you want to please God?

- Because you hate sin?

- Because Jesus died so that you
  could be forgiven?

Pray!

Pray that you will LOVE and OBEY
God more. Look back at the Ten
Commandments. Pick one you
really need God's help with and
talk to Him about it.

Promise keeper

**Exodus
24 v 1-8**

*God has given
the Israelites
the Ten
Commandments
and some other
laws too (they
are in Exodus 20
v 22 – 23 v 33).*

Here are three possible reactions to God's commands.

God can't tell me what to do!

I try my best to obey most of them.

I'll do everything God wants me to.

Think!

Which of those is most like how you feel after reading the Ten Commandments?

_____

_____

Read Exodus 24 v 1-3

Now tick the speech bubble that shows what the Israelites said about God's commands. And they really meant it! They even made a special agreement with God to prove it.

Read verses 4-8

God had promised...

If you keep my commands, I will bless you and destroy all your enemies.

The people promised...

Everything that the Lord has commanded, we will do. We will be obedient (v 7).

What's this special agreement called? Write down the <u>underlined</u> letters to find out.

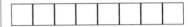

A **covenant** is a special agreement that must not be broken. This covenant was between God and His people. God **always** kept His part of the covenant. He took care of the Israelites and kept all of His promises to them.

The Israelites promised to obey **everything** God had said.

Do you think they will keep their promise?

Yes/No _____

WEIRD WORDS

Nadab & Abihu
Aaron's sons

Elders
Leaders

Altar
Table where gifts of meat to God (burnt offerings) were put

Sacrificed
Killed

Book of the covenant
The laws mentioned in Exodus chapters 20 – 23

Pray!

Thank God that He **always** keeps His promises to us, even though we let Him down so often.

Blood test

**Hebrews
9 v 19-22**

*Remember what
we read about
yesterday?*

*Read Exodus
24 v 3-8 again.*

*Which word
appears three
times in v6-8?*

B_____

WEIRD WORDS

Scarlet
Bright red

Hyssop
A bushy plant

Scroll
What the laws were
written on

Tabernacle
Tent where God was
present

Cleansed
Purified

What has blood got to do with making a covenant agreement?

It was a sign to show that they really meant it. We still use special signs to confirm agreements today.

Let's shake on it!

The blood was a sign to teach God's people a special lesson.

Find it in Hebrews 9 v 19-22

The reason why Moses sprinkled everything in blood was to teach them... what?

Put the letters with numbers under them in the right place.

WITHOUT THE
1   2

SHEDDING OF BLOOD
3 4   5 6   7

THERE IS NEVER...
8   9

___ ___ ___ ___ ___ ___ ___ ___ ___ ___ ___
7 2 8 6 1 9 4 5 4 3 3

(The answer's in v22)

The Israelites would need to be forgiven loads in the future. They often disobeyed God, and failed to stick to their side of the covenant agreement. But the blood was a special sign of how they could still be forgiven.

But how? Whose **blood** can forgive sins???

The blood of J__ __ __ __

Wow!

We've all failed to keep God's commands. We've all sinned. But there is still hope for us if we trust entirely in the blood of Jesus for forgiveness!

What's that mean?

It means that Jesus bled and died on the cross to take the punishment we deserve for disobeying God. So that if we trust in Jesus and say sorry, we can be forgiven for all our wrongs! Jesus shed His blood so that we can be forgiven!

> For a free e-booklet on why
> Jesus died, email
> discover@thegoodbook.co.uk
> or check out
> www.thegoodbook.co.uk/contact-us
> to find our UK mailing address.

Close encounter

Exodus 24 v 9-18

Moses, Aaron and 70 Israelite leaders went up Mount Sinai to meet God!

WEIRD WORDS

Lapis lazuli
Blue gemstone

Tablets
Large stones

Dispute
Argument

Glory of the LORD
A glimpse of God's greatness

Consuming fire
A very dangerous fire that destroys anything near it

Read Exodus 24 v 9-11

These people had an amazing glimpse of how great and beautiful and powerful God is!

Read verses 12-17

Only Moses had the special privilege of staying with God at the top of the mountain (Joshua probably only went part of the way). But it wasn't going to be easy for Moses.

Would you have gone to the top of that mountain?

YES/NO _____

Would you have been scared?

YES/NO _____

Moses knew that God had called Him. He could trust God not to harm Him.

Would you have waited for 6 days while nothing happened?

YES/NO _____

Moses was patient and waited for God's time to speak.

Read verse 18

Would you have walked into the burning cloud?

YES/NO _____

Moses knew it was the only way of obeying God and the only way to be close to God. So he did it.

Would you have stayed alone with God for 40 days?

YES/NO _____

Moses knew that there is nothing better than to have God close to us. 40 days wouldn't have seemed too long to Moses!

Think!

Christians won't get to see God as Moses did until they go to live with Him.

But God has promised to ALWAYS be with His people. He has given His Holy Spirit to live in Christians, helping them to obey Him. God is ALWAYS close to Christians!

Pray!

Thank God that even though He's so powerful and holy, He still wants us to have a close relationship with Him!

Revelation: Jesus revealed

Revelation
1 v 1-3

Today we start a new book, called Revelation.

It's full of visions of thrones, lampstands, scrolls, colourful horses, earthquakes, trumpets, angels, beasts, a lamb and a dragon!

But it's all about JESUS!!

WEIRD WORDS

Testifies
Gives evidence

Testimony
What Jesus said

Prophecy
Message from God

Read Revelation 1 v 1-2

This is a letter written by the disciple John. He's the one who wrote the book called *John*, which we'll be reading later in this issue. He introduces Revelation himself...

> This is the revelation from J_____
> C_____

Revelation means **revealing** something. This book is a message from Jesus!

> ...to show His
> s_____ what
> must _____
> _____ (v1)

This book is for Jesus' servants — that's all Christians! And it's about important stuff that is **going to happen**. And also stuff that **has happened** and stuff that is **happening now**!

Read verse 3

What does John say about people who read this book and take it to heart?

> They are
> b_____

Most Bibles say **blessed**. (The Good News Bible says *happy*!) Blessed means more than just happy. It means... *(fill in the top half of each letter to find out)*

SPECIALLY

FAVOURED BY GOD

Sounds pretty good. So how can we benefit from reading Revelation? **Verse 3** tells us.

1. R_____d it!

2. H_____r it!

3. _____ what is written in it!

Pray!

Ask God to help you take to heart the things you read in this book. And that you'll learn loads more about Jesus!

26

**Revelation
1 v 4-8**

*We're reading
John's great
letter to
Christians in
Asia Minor (part
of Turkey).*

*It's all about
Jesus...*

WEIRD WORDS

Province
Area

Grace
God giving us far
more than we
deserve

Glory
Honour and respect

Pierced
Wounded

Mourn
Be very upset

Almighty
God

Fantastic facts

How does John greet the Christians
he's writing to?

Read Revelation 1 v 4-5

*What does John pray that these
Christians will enjoy?*

Fill in the vowels (aeiou)...

Gr__c__ and p__ __c__ from
h__m who __s and w__s
and __s to c__m__ (v4)

Wow!

God has always existed! He always
will exist! And He's in control of the
whole universe right now! He brings
peace to all Christians — they're
comforted by the knowledge they
will live with Him for ever! He gives
them far more than they deserve!

Seven spirits (v4)

In Revelation, **seven** is a special
number. It crops up 54 times in the
book! It stands for perfection and
completeness. So seven spirits =
God's one perfect spirit — the **Holy
Spirit.**

What else does John say?

Read verse 8

Alpha and Omega are A and Z in
the Greek alphabet. God is the first
and the last: **He is the God of all
time and history!**

So what do we learn about Jesus?

Read verses 5-7

**He is the f__ __thf__l
w__tn__ss**
Jesus brought us the truth

F__rstb__rn from the dead
God brought Jesus back to life and
put Him in charge

**The r__l__r of the k__ngs
of the earth**
Jesus is ruler of the world!

**He l__v__s us and fr__ __d us
from our s__ns!**
That's true for all Christians

**And He's made Christians
into a k__ngd__m to s__rv__
G__d the Father!**
That's what we should be doing
right now

**He will return again at the
end of history (v7)**

Pray!

Read through those facts about
Jesus. Now go through them
again, praising and thanking Him
for each one.

ⅠⅠ

Tell a vision

*Revelation is
all about God
revealing the
amazing truth
about Jesus.*

*He revealed this
to John in several
visions.*

*Today, John starts
to tell us about
his first vision.*

WEIRD WORDS

**Patient
endurance**
Putting up with
hassle

Testimony
What he said

In the Spirit
I don't know what
that means!

Read Revelation 1 v 9

Where was John?

Island of Thermos ☐

Island of Patmos ☐

A pile of compost ☐

He was there because of...

the word of God ☐

the worm of Nod and a pile
of compost ☐

the word of God and the
testimony of Jesus ☐

Patmos was a prison island. John
was sent there by the Romans
because they hated him preaching
about Jesus.

What did John have in common
with the people he was writing
to?

Suffering ☐

Serving God as part
of His Kingdom ☐

Patient endurance ☐

All three! They were all suffering
persecution and hassle for telling
people about Jesus. But they were
patiently coping with it. And they
were living with God as King of their
lives.

Read verses 10-11

When did John see the vision?

The Lord's Day (Sunday) ☐

Easter ☐

5th November ☐

What did he hear?

Loud voice like a terrapin ☐

Loud vole like a trombone ☐

Loud voice like a trumpet ☐

What did it say?

Write what you hear ☐

See what you write ☐

Write what you see ☐

John did write down the amazing
things he saw. We'll start reading
about them tomorrow...

Pray!

Ask God to help you...
a) tell people about Jesus
b) cope with any hassle you get
   for it
c) live with Him as King of your
   life

28

**Revelation
1 v 12-16**

lampstand

*Yesterday we
read that John
heard a loud
voice like a
trumpet.*

But who was it?

*John turned
around and an
awesome sight
met his eyes...*

Son shining

Read Revelation 1 v 12-16

*John says he saw **someone like a
son of man**. Who do you think it was?*

Check out John 3 v 10-15

The **Son of Man** is how Jesus referred to Himself.
So John is seeing a vision of Jesus.
Use the word pool to fill in the gaps in the verses from Revelation.

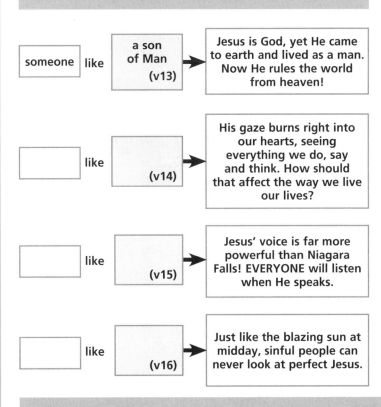

someone   voice   eyes
the sun shining   rushing waters   face
a Son of Man   blazing fire

| someone | like | **a son of Man** (v13) | → | **Jesus is God, yet He came to earth and lived as a man. Now He rules the world from heaven!** |

| | like | (v14) | → | **His gaze burns right into our hearts, seeing everything we do, say and think. How should that affect the way we live our lives?** |

| | like | (v15) | → | **Jesus' voice is far more powerful than Niagara Falls! EVERYONE will listen when He speaks.** |

| | like | (v16) | → | **Just like the blazing sun at midday, sinful people can never look at perfect Jesus.** |

Pray! What an incredible description of Jesus!
What does that make you want to say to Him?

Keys of death

**Revelation
1 v 17-20**

John is seeing an awesome vision of Jesus in all His glory!

Let's find out more about Jesus Christ...

WEIRD WORDS

Living One
God, who is alive and who gives life

Hades
Hell

For all of today's missing words, go back one letter (B=A, C=B etc).

Read Revelation 1 v 17

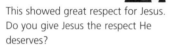

K P I O

G F M M   B U

,

K F T V T   G F F U

Think!

This showed great respect for Jesus. Do you give Jesus the respect He deserves?

What did Jesus say?

J   B N   U I F

G J S T U   B O E

U I F   M B T U

Wow!

Jesus has always been around, and always will be around! Jesus is God!

Read verse 18

I have power over

E F   B U I   B O E

I B E F T

Wow!

Jesus has defeated death and hell! So His followers don't need to fear death. Sin is not in control of their lives any more — Jesus is!

Read verses 19-20

K F T V T   J T

M P S E   P G

U I F   D I V S D I

Wow!

The church is all Christians everywhere! Jesus holds them in His hands! He's in control of their lives and their future!

Pray!

Read through today's page again and find things to thank God for.

30

**Revelation
2 v 1-7**

*In John's vision,
Jesus told him
to write to
seven churches.*

*Jesus has four
things to say
to Ephesus, the
first church...*

WEIRD WORDS

Perseverance
Keeping going

Apostles
Teachers sent by
Jesus

Hardships
Tough times

Forsaken
Abandoned

Repent
Turn away from
wrong things you
do

Fuss in Ephesus

1. PRAISE FOR WHAT THEY'VE DONE
Read Revelation 2 v 1-3, 6

The Ephesian Christians work hard
for God. They've not been fooled by
liars and false teachers (Nicolaitans
— v6). And they've not let hard
times stop them serving God.

Action!

How can you work hard
for God this week?

_____

_____

_____

_____

2. CRITICISM OF WHAT THEY'VE DONE WRONG
Read verse 4

They don't love Jesus (or each other)
as much as when they first became
Christians.

Think!

Are you as enthusiastic about Jesus
as you used to be?

3. INSTRUCTIONS!
Read verse 5

They have to turn away from their
wrong ways. They need to start
showing their love for Jesus again,
or Jesus will let their church die out.

Action!

What will you do this week to show
your love for Jesus and for other
Christians?

_____

_____

_____

4. A HUGE PROMISE!
Read verse 7

Look what Jesus promises to people
who obey His instructions and live
for Him! It sounds confusing, but
He's saying that they will enjoy a
great life with God for ever!

Pray!

What have you written down
today? Ask God to help you do
those things this week. And ask
Him to help you love Him more
and more.

Nice little Smyrna

**Revelation
2 v 8-11**

*Christians in the
town of Smyrna
are having a
tough time.*

*What does Jesus
say to them?*

Afflictions
Problems

Poverty
Having no money

Slander
Telling lies about
someone

Persecution
Hassle for being
followers of Jesus

Faithful
Obeying God, living
His way

Victor
Winner

Second death
Hell

1. PRAISE FOR WHAT THEY'VE DONE
Read Revelation 2 v 8-10

Certain Jews (Jesus calls them the
synagogue of Satan) are saying
untrue things about the Christians
in Smyrna. These Christians are
also poor. Yet Jesus tells them that
they're actually rich!

*Put a big **R** in the boxes which show
why these Christians are rich in
God's sight (v9).*

> **They have little money**

> **They are promised
> eternal life — a
> victor's crown!**

> **They are standing up
> for their belief in Jesus**

> **They sold expensive
> sandals**

> **Jesus has saved them
> from sin**

As far as God is concerned, these
people are rich in the only way that
matters! They will live forever with
Him!

2. CRITICISM OF WHAT THEY'VE DONE WRONG

Jesus doesn't have any!

3. INSTRUCTIONS!
Read verse 10

Some of the guys in Smyrna will get
hassled for being Christians. Some
will be thrown into prison. And
some might even be killed!
But Jesus tells them to keep
following Him. They don't need
to be afraid.

> **Why?**

4. A HUGE PROMISE!
Read verses 10-11

Jesus promises great things to those
who stick with Him. They will be
given life as their victor's crown
(v10). That's eternal life with God!
And they won't have to face the
second death — punishment in hell.
Great news!

Pray!

From the list below, pick things to
talk to God about:

- Being hassled for your faith
- The promise of eternal life
- Friends who aren't Christians
- Riches you can thank God for

Talk to God in prayer right now!

32

Revelation 3 v 14-22

We've been reading Jesus' messages to seven different churches. We don't have time for all seven, so let's jump to the last one...

Take your temperature

1. PRAISE FOR WHAT THEY'VE DONE

Sadly, Jesus doesn't have any. These Christians are not serving Him as they should be doing.

2. CRITICISM OF WHAT THEY'VE DONE WRONG
Read Revelation 3 v 14-17

Being **lukewarm** doesn't sound so bad. But these Christians are taking it easy, not serving God with their whole lives. That's not good enough for Jesus!

And they think they're fine, because they're rich. But Jesus tells them that they're miserable, poor and blind! They seem comfortable and happy, but they're ignoring God and not working hard for Him.

Think!

Have you gone lukewarm? Has anything become more important to you than Jesus?

Money? Friends? Sport? Add some of your own.

_____

_____

_____

_____

3. INSTRUCTIONS!
Read verses 18-19

Jesus still loves these Christians! What does He tell them to do? Add the vowels (aeiou) to find out...

1. B__y g__ld fr__m m__

2. and wh__t__ cl__th__s

3. and ointment
   f__r y__ __r __y__s

Jesus is saying, *Don't look to earthly things for happiness. Come to me for everything you need.*

Action!

What will you do to put Jesus first in your life?

_____

_____

_____

4. A HUGE PROMISE!
Read verses 20-22

Jesus wants to be close friends with anyone who'll welcome Him as ruler of their life! (v20)

Pray!

Say sorry to Jesus for being lukewarm. Turn to Him for anything you need. Ask Him to be your best friend.

WEIRD WORDS

The Amen
Jesus

Wretched
Pathetic

Refined
Made pure

Salve
Ointment

Rebuke
Tell off

Earnest
Serious about something

33

Heaven's above

Revelation 4 v 1-11

John is telling us what God showed Him in an amazing vision.

Want a sneaky peek at heaven?

WEIRD WORDS

Jasper and ruby
Beautiful jewels

Seven spirits of God
In Revelation, the number seven stands for completeness and perfection. So this means God's perfect Holy Spirit.

Holy
Perfect, pure.

Read Revelation 4 v 1-6

Wow, what an amazing sight! God on His throne in heaven!

And lots of strange things are happening. They remind us of some of the great things God did in Old Testament times.

Look up the Old Testament verses, then match them with the things from John's vision.

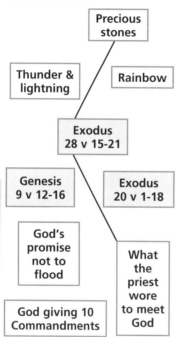

Wow!

God was faithful to His people in Old Testament times, and He still is! This great God is King for all time. Is He the King of your life?

Read verses 6-11

The **24 elders** stand for all of God's people — Christians.

The **four living creatures** stand for everything God has created. So John sees **all of creation** worshipping God!

What are their reasons for worshipping God? (v8, v11)

_____

_____

_____

_____

_____

_____

_____

Pray!

Now spend some time thanking and worshipping God for these great truths about Him.

Scroll with it

Today John tells us more amazing things from his vision of heaven.

There's an angel, a lion, a lamb with seven horns and seven eyes...

And a scroll that is impossible to open...

Read Revelation 5 v 1-4

This scroll contains God's plan for world history. God's plan to punish sin. God's plan to rescue His people from sin.

But no one can open the scroll. So no one can carry out God's perfect plan. No one can deal with sin. No wonder John is sobbing his heart out! (v4)

Read verses 5-7

Who is this person described as both a lion and a lamb? ? ?
Who's the only one who can open the scroll? The only one who can carry out God's plan to deal with sin?

Who is most like a lion ~ a powerful King? (John 12 v 12-13)

_E_ _ _ _

Who is a descendant of King David? (Matthew 1 v 6~17)

_ _S_ _ _

Who was described as the Lamb of God? (John 1 v 29)

_ _ _ _U_ _

Who died, but still lives? (Romans 1 v 4)

_ _ _ _S

Seven horns = great power! Who is all-powerful?

J_ _ _ _ _

Wow!

Get the picture? Only JESUS can open the scroll. Jesus put God's plan into action. The plan to save us from our sins! Thank God for sending Jesus to carry out His perfect plans.

Singing praises

The only one who can open the scroll is the lamb.

Only He can put God's plan into action.

God's plan to rescue us from sin!

The lamb is **Jesus**. Only He can rescue us from our sins.

Read Revelation 5 v 7-14

What an amazing sound!

Who is praising Jesus? Find the answers in the wordsearch.

A	Y	F	E	A	R	T	H	B	E
L	J	O	O	P	X	H	L	Q	V
I	G	U	H	E	F	O	D	H	N
V	C	R	E	A	T	U	R	E	S
I	H	K	A	G	D	S	C	L	T
N	B	A	V	I	S	A	Z	D	I
G	X	O	E	N	F	N	A	E	U
T	W	E	N	T	Y	D	R	R	K
C	A	N	G	E	L	S	B	S	J

FOUR L_____
C_____ (v8)

T_____-F_____
E_____ (v8)

T_____
OF A_____ (v11)

EVERY CREATURE IN
H_____
AND E_____ (v13)

Read verses 9-10 again

Look at what they say to Jesus!

> You were killed and by your death you purchased people for God!

THE BAD NEWS

We've all sinned and disobeyed God. We all belong to sin. It has a grip on our lives.

THE GOOD NEWS

Only Jesus could buy us back. He paid the ultimate price by dying on the cross in our place. Everyone who trusts in Jesus has been bought back by Him. They now belong to God!

Action!

If you're a Christian, write on spare paper how you can show that you belong to God. How can you serve Him?

Pray!

Will you join in praising Jesus right now? You can use verses 9-14 to help you!

**Revelation
6 v 1-8**

*The scroll
describes
the time
between Jesus'
resurrection and
His return to
earth one day.*

*That time is
right now.*

Horse code

The scroll tells us a lot about the world we live in...

Read Revelation 6 v 1-4

... and give the horses the correct colours!

The first horse (v2) stands for military leaders invading other countries.

The second horse (v4) stands for war and violence.

*These things are happening **right now**. Write down two examples of violence and war in the world.*

> 1.
>
> 2.

Read verses 5-6

The third horse comes with the announcement that grain will cost 10 times the normal price! This horse stands for famine.

Read verses 7-8

The fourth horse stands for death. And hell is following close behind.

Write down examples of famine and death in the world.

> 1.
>
> 2.

Terrible things like this are happening right now. But who is in control? (See verses 1,3,5,7)

>

Wow!

Sometimes it may seem as if evil is in control of the world. But Jesus (the Lamb) has already beaten sin and death. He's in control!

Pray!

... about the things you've written down. Ask God to do something amazing in those situations.

37

Performing seals

Time to open the fifth and sixth seals on the scroll.

They reveal more terrifying events...

WEIRD WORDS

Altar
Table where gifts to God were put

Testimony
Telling people about Jesus

Sovereign
In control of everything

Avenge
Get revenge

Wrath
Anger and punishment

Read Revelation 6 v 9-11

It's a fact: Christians get hassled and picked on for their belief in Jesus. For me and you, it's probably only a bit of teasing.

But in other parts of the world, people are put in prison or even killed for being Christians.

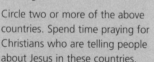

Bangladesh	**Turkey**
Iran **Syria**	**Egypt**
Pakistan	**Laos**
North Korea	**Sudan**

Pray!

Circle two or more of the above countries. Spend time praying for Christians who are telling people about Jesus in these countries.

**For more info
on Christians suffering
around the world, check
out the *Christian Solidarity
Worldwide* website:
www.csw.org.uk**

It's amazing when Christians continue telling people about Jesus, even when it might lead to them being attacked or worse.

But look at verse 11. God gives them white robes as a sign of victory and having their sins wiped clean by God!

And God will punish those who refuse to live for Him...

Read verses 12-17

Wow!

Terrifying. One day, Jesus will return to end the world. He will punish everyone who has turned against Him.

Two very different outcomes for two sets of people. Those who **live for God**, and those who **reject Him**.

Fill in the gaps from

Romans 6 v 23

Th__ w_g_s _f s_n
_s d__ __th, b_t th__
g_ft _f G_d _s
_t_rn_l l_fe _n
Chr__st J_s_s.

**Talk to God about how
you feel.**

**Revelation
7 v 1-8**

Yesterday, we
read about
God's anger
and punishment
against people
who won't live
for Him.

But it's not all
bad news!

Read Revelation
6 v 17.

**The terrible
day of God's
anger is here!**

**Who can
stand up to
it? Who can
survive it?**

Safe and sound

Today we'll find out who can.

Read Revelation 7 v 1-2

*Now fill in the gaps. See if you can
do it from memory, then check with
the verses.*

**There were four
_____ standing at
four _____ of
the _____. They
were holding back the four
_____ to stop them
from destroying the earth.
The four _____
had been given power to
_____ the
_____ and
_____.**

Why does God stop the angels
destroying the world?

Read verses 3-8

God's servants (Christians) had seals
put on their heads (v3).

You've probably seen cows or sheep
with numbers on them to show who
owns them. Seals were a similar
idea. So the seals on the heads of
these people show that they belong
to God and that He will protect
them!

144,000

It doesn't mean exactly 144,000
people will be safe. 144,000 stands
for the huge and complete crowd
of people that God will keep safe. It
stands for all of His people!

EXTRA!

Notice the 12 tribes of Israel from
the Old Testament (v5-8). "Israel"
now stands for everyone who
believes in Jesus. Old Testament
believers and Christians too. God
loves them and keeps them safe.

The world won't be destroyed until
God has gathered up all His people
and made them safe (v3). That's
who can survive God's anger! His
people! Christians!

Pray!

If Jesus has rescued you from
your sin, you are safe! You
belong to God! Want to thank
Him loads??? If you're not yet a
Christian, will you ask Jesus to
rescue you?

Raise the praise!

**Revelation
7 v 9-17**

*Yesterday, we
saw how God's
people are
protected by God
from His anger.*

*Today, we get to
see God's people
in heaven!*

WEIRD WORDS

Multitude
Massive crowd

Salvation
Rescuing people
from their sins

Tribulation
Times of suffering
and persecution for
following Jesus

Read Revelation 7 v 9-12

*What are God's people praising Him
for? (v10)*

S _ _ _ _ _ _ _ _ n

This means that God rescued them
from sin! (More on this later...)

This is such an amazing gift from
God! That's why everyone in heaven
is praising God so much (see v12).

Think!

Do you give God the praise and
thanks He deserves? Maybe you
could use v12 to help you...

Read verses 13-17

This is a brilliant description of
God's people — Christians. They
have come through tough times of
persecution for serving God.

*Fill in the gaps, to show how else
Christians are described.*

Washed in the b_ _ _ _d
of the l_ _b (v14)

Remember who the Lamb is? It's
Jesus! By His blood (death on the
cross), Christians have had all their
sins washed away! Their sins have
been totally forgiven by Jesus.

Never again will they
h_ _ _ _r or
t_ _ _ _t (v16)

God will protect His people. They
will go to live with Him for ever.
And they will never suffer again!

Jesus will be their
Sh_ _ _ _ _d (v17)

The Lamb who died for them will
become their Shepherd! Jesus will
look after Christians and lead them.

Pray!

Read through this brilliant
description again. If you're a
Christian, then you've got LOADS
to thank God for!! Use today's
verses to help you praise and
thank God.

Email us with any questions about Revelation: discover@thegoodbook.co.uk

Jesus: Unbeatable love

**John
13 v 1-5**

*We're now
going to jump
into the story
of Jesus' life, as
told by John.
(The same John
who wrote
Revelation!)*

*It's getting
towards the end
of Jesus' time
on earth.*

*And Jesus
knows it...*

WEIRD WORDS

**Passover
Festival**

Festival to
remember the
time God rescued
His people from
slavery in Egypt

Jesus knows He is soon going to...

• be betrayed by a friend

• suffer and die on the cross

• go to be with His Father in heaven

So He's probably worrying about
what's going to happen to Him,
right? Wrong!

Read John 13 v 1

*Who was Jesus thinking about?
Unscramble the anagrams.*

_____ _____

I S H   N O W

That's His disciples! Jesus spent the
last evening before He died showing
how much He loved His friends. Isn't
that awesome?!

Think!

Do you need to spend more time
with your Christian friends? Who
could you spend more time with?

_____

_____

_____

_____

_____

Read verses 4-5

How would you like to do that?! To
get down on your knees and wash
your friends' dirty feet?! Disgusting!
But Jesus didn't complain because
He loved His disciples.

Action!

What can YOU do to show love for
your friends?

_____

_____

_____

Go on then, do it!

Now read verses 2-3

Jesus knew that He was going to
die. And it was in His power to
either stop it or go along with it.
He willingly went to die for you and
me! That's how He would show His
love for all of us.

Pray!

Want to say THANK YOU?

**John
13 v 6-17**

*Jesus is washing
His disciples'
grubby feet!*

*Imagine what
it would be like
to have the
Lord Jesus doing
something so
humiliating for
you.*

*Maybe you'd feel
a bit like Peter...*

Foot notes

Read John 13 v 6-11

Wow!

Jesus washed His disciples' feet as
a picture of something far more
amazing. It was to show that Jesus
would wash their sins away. He
would forgive them for all the
wrong stuff they had done. And
He'll do the same for us if we ask!

*Peter asked Jesus to wash his whole
body (v9)! Cross out every third
letter to find out what Jesus was
saying to Peter.*

**YOTUHHAVEEASLREEAL
DYEBETENTWAESHREDS
FRSOMHYOOURUSILNSDY
OBUOENLCYNREEODYSOU
SRFEEEDTWOASUHITNG**

Y_ _   _ _ _ _ _

_ _ _ _ _ _ _

_ _ _ _

_ _ _ _ _ _ _

_ _ _ _   _ _ _ _

_ _ _ _ _.   Y_ _

_ _ _ _   _ _ _ _

_ _ _ _ _ _ _.

Being washed all over is a picture
of being forgiven for all the wrong
things we'll ever do. That happens
when we trust in Jesus.

Washing feet is a picture of saying
sorry to God each time we sin,
remembering that through Jesus
we've been forgiven.

Read verses 12-17

Action!

On a sheet of paper, make a *HELP
LIST*. Write down the names of
family, friends and people from
church. Next to their names, write
down what you can do for each of
them this week (e.g. polish shoes,
help with homework, clean church).
Don't write down stuff you usually
do anyway!

Pray!

Ask God to help you serve those
people over the next few weeks.
And thank God for sending Jesus
to wash away our sins.

Jesus in control

42

John 13 v 18-30

Jesus is eating His last meal with His disciples before His death.

Read John 13 v 18-20

Jesus knew that one of His closest friends would betray Him. He told the disciples this so that, after it happened, they'd finally realise that Jesus was **God's Son**, and was in control all along.

Think!

Do you believe that Jesus is God's Son?

	1	2	3	4	5
a	V	J	T	J	R
b	N	E	U	B	L
c	D	D	L	A	M
d	B	W	A	E	V
e	N	R	C	S	L

The traitor was

— — — — —

Verse 27 says that the devil (Satan) entered Judas. The devil was behind the plot to kill Jesus.

But Jesus was in charge. Everything that happened to Him, He allowed to happen. He knew that He had to die so that our sins could be washed away.

Read verses 21-30

*Reveal the traitor by circling **True** or **False** for these statements. Then circle the right letters in the grid.*

	T	F
Jesus was happy (v21)	a 5	b 3
The disciples were confused (v22)	e 4	b 2
Jesus gave the traitor some bread(v26)	a 2	d 1
Jesus tried to stop him	e 2	d 3
The disciples knew(v28) who the traitor was	c 4	c 2

Pray!

Thank Jesus for going through such sadness for you.

For the free e-booklet *Why did Jesus die?*, email discover@thegoodbook.co.uk or check out www.thegoodbook.co.uk/contact-us to find our UK mailing address.

WEIRD WORDS

Scripture
Old Testament

Troubled in spirit
Really upset

Testified
Spoke an important truth

Disciple who Jesus loved
Probably John, who wrote the book we're reading

Glory story

43

**John
13 v 31-38**

Jesus has been eating His last meal with His disciples.

Jesus knows that His friend Judas will betray Him and hand Him over to His enemies.

WEIRD WORDS

Son of Man
Jesus. As well as being God's Son, He was a human being

Glorified
Shown to be perfect

Disown
Pretend not to know me

What was going to happen to Jesus then?

Jesus was going to die on the cross before going back to heaven.

That sounds awful.

That's not how Jesus described it.

Read John 13 v 31-32

So Jesus was going to be gl_____!

Jesus would be betrayed, rejected, insulted, hated and killed. How could that be a good thing?

God sent His Son, Jesus, to die on the cross in our place so that we can have our sins forgiven. It shows us how great and loving God is. And it shows that Jesus really is God's Son.

So what would happen to the disciples?

Read verses 33, 36-38

They couldn't f_____ Jesus to heaven yet (v36). P_____ didn't understand, and thought he could follow Jesus (v37). But he didn't realise how weak he was. He would deny knowing Jesus t_____ times (v38)!

Read verses 34-35

How should Jesus' followers (Christians) treat each other?

They should l_____ each o_____ just as J_____ has shown great l_____ for them!
That's how Christians should be recognised — showing love to each other.

Think & pray!

How can you show love for other people? Have you done any of the things you wrote down two days ago?
Thank Jesus for loving you so much that He died for you. Ask Him to help you show love to people around you.

44

**John
14 v 1-3**

Jesus has just told His disciples that He's leaving them.

And they won't be able to go with Him...

Going home

How do you think the disciples were feeling?

But what did Jesus tell them?

Read John 14 v 1

Don't let your hearts be
__ __ __ __ __ __ __ __

Jesus told them three things to cheer them up!

Read verses 2-3

1. Jesus is going to His
__ __ __ __ __ __ __ ,
__ __ __ __ __ __

Even when Jesus died, His disciples wouldn't need to worry. Jesus was on His way home to His Father in heaven.

2. Jesus is going to prepare
__ __ __ __ __ __ __ __ __
__ __ __ __ __ __

That's why Jesus was leaving them. By dying on the cross, He would make it possible for them to live with Him for ever!

3. Jesus is going to
__ __ __ __ __ __ __
__ __ __ __ __ __

We don't know **when** Jesus will come back. But we know that He **will** come back. And He will make sure that every single one of His followers (Christians) will go to live with Him for ever!

Pray!

Is there anything from today's reading you want to praise and thank Jesus for?

A	B	C	D	E	F	H	K	L	M	O	P	R	S	T	U

One way only

**John
14 v 4-6**

Jesus has told His disciples that He's going to leave them.

But they shouldn't worry, because one day they'll go to live with Him for ever.

Thomas, one of the disciples, was baffled. Read his conversation with Jesus and fill in the missing vowels (aeiou).

Read John 14 v 4-6

Y_ _ kn__w
th__ w__y t_ th__
pl_c_ wh_r_
I __m g_ __ng.

L_rd, w_ d__n't
kn__w wh__r_ yo__
ar_ g_ __ng.
So h__w c_n w_
kn__w th__ w__y?

I __m th__ w__y
__nd th__ tr__th __nd
th__ l_f_. N__ __n__
c_m_s t_ th__
F__th__r __xc_pt
thr__ __gh m__.

Jesus doesn't just show us the way to God. He *is* the way to God! He died on the cross to make it possible for us to be forgiven and live for ever with Him.

Jesus doesn't just tell us the truth about God. He *is* the truth about God! He is God.

Jesus doesn't just give LIFE to His people. He *is* life! He's the point of our lives. The one we should live for.

Read verse 6 again

Accepting Jesus and being forgiven by Him is the **ONLY** way to get to live with God. Being a good person isn't good enough. Following other gods or rules or superstitions isn't good enough.

Want to know more about accepting Jesus and being forgiven by Him? Then email us for the free e-booklet WHAT'S IT ALL ABOUT?	**Got friends who don't believe that Jesus is the ONLY way to heaven? Then email us for the free fact sheet on TELLING YOUR FRIENDS ABOUT JESUS.**

Email
discover@thegoodbook.co.uk
or check out
www.thegoodbook.co.uk/contact-us
to find our UK mailing address.

John
14 v 7-11

Philip

Jesus says that He is the only way to get to know God.

But the disciples still haven't worked out exactly who Jesus is...

Philip flustered

It's Philip's turn to be confused.

Read John 14 v 7-9

Cross out all the Bs, Cs and Js to reveal what Jesus said (v7).

BIFYCJOUJJRECCALBJB
LBYKJNOCBWMEBYOCU
WICJLJLKNBBOWCMJY
FCJATBHERCASWBELLJ

If _____

_____

_____

_____

1. Knowing Jesus is knowing God

If you know Jesus and trust Him to forgive your sins, then you know God too!

Read verses 10-11

2. Jesus' words are God's words

Want to know what God has to say to **you**? Then check out Jesus' words in the Bible. Here are a few to start with...

John 3 v 16-21
John 10 v 11-18
John 13 v 34-35

3. Jesus' actions are God's actions

God sent Jesus into the world. All the amazing things Jesus did are what God wanted Him to do. When Jesus died for us, it was because God sent Him to die for us. So that we can have our sins forgiven by Him.

Pray!

Spend time talking to God now. Thank Him that you know Him and can talk to Him.
Thank Him for all that Jesus said and all that Jesus has done in your life.

47

**John
14 v 12-14**

*Get ready for
some more
surprising words
from Jesus...*

It's a miracle!

*Name some of the miracles that
Jesus did:*

_____

_____

_____

_____

Read John 14 v 12

> **What? We'll do
> even greater miracles
> than Jesus? No way!**

When Jesus said this, He was about
to leave His disciples to be with His
Father in heaven. But Jesus wouldn't
leave them all alone. He would give
all believers His Holy Spirit to help
them serve God and do amazing
things for Him. (More about that
tomorrow!)

Amazingly, Christians nowadays can
probably tell more people about
God than Jesus did 2000 years ago.
But it's Jesus' Holy Spirit that helps
us to do it.

WEIRD WORDS

Works
Miracles

Glorified
Given the praise,
honour and respect
that God deserves

Read verses 13-14

*Rearrange the word blocks to reveal
Jesus' awesome promise.*

will	ask	I	whatever

my	do	name	you	in

I			

Wow!

If we want to serve God, Jesus will
help us do it!

We can ask God to help us with
whatever He wants us to do for
Him. And He will!

Action!

How could you serve God more?

_____

_____

_____

_____

Pray!

Ask God to help you to serve Him
in these ways. Ask Him to use you
to bring glory to Him.

Heavenly helper

48

**John
14 v 15-20**

Do you love Jesus? How do you show it?

_____

_____

_____

_____

Read John 14 v 15

Loving Jesus means obeying what He says in the Bible.

More about that tomorrow...

WEIRD WORDS

Advocate
Helper

Spirit of truth
Holy Spirit

But Jesus was about to leave His disciples. For three whole years they had been with Him and had devoted their lives to Him. Surely He wouldn't leave them now???

Jesus said He was going back to His Father in heaven. So would He leave His disciples alone?

YES/NO _____

Read His promise in verse 18

... and unjumble the anagrams.

I will not l_____

e v a l e

you as o_____.

r a n s h o p

I will c_____ to you.

m e c o

Hold on! Jesus was going back to heaven, so how could He be with His disciples?

Read verses 16-17

God would send them a new helper — **the Spirit**.

The Spirit of truth

That's the **Holy Spirit**. The Holy Spirit is God. When Jesus went back to heaven, He gave His Spirit to live in the lives of all believers (Christians). The Holy Spirit helps us to live for God.

What does the Holy Spirit do?

The Holy Spirit...

- **teaches us the truth about God (v17)**
- **reminds us of Jesus' words (v26)**
- **helps us tell people about Jesus (John 15 v 26-27)**
- **makes people realise they've sinned (16 v 7-8)**
- **will be with Christians for ever! (14 v 16)**

Read verses 19-20

Jesus doesn't leave His followers on their own. They have the Holy Spirit helping them to serve God with their lives! And one day, they will live with Jesus for ever!

Pray!

Thank God that you're not on your own! Thank Him for the incredible gift of the Holy Spirit to help you live for Him.

49

**John
14 v 21-24**

*Who do you
love? Who do you
really care for?*

_____
_____
_____
_____

*How do you show
that you love
them?*

_____
_____
_____
_____
_____

Now for the big question we
touched on yesterday...

Love lessons

Do you love Jesus?

Yes! ☐

No, not really ☐

I want to... ☐

Not enough ☐

What does it mean to love Jesus?
How do we show our love for Him?

Read John 14 v 21

People who love Jesus...

do what they like ☐

wear Christian t-shirts ☐

keep (obey) His
commands ☐

**If you love Jesus, what does He
promise you?**

God the Father loves you ☐

Jesus loves you ☐

Both of those are true!

And that's not all...

Read verses 22-24

> **How come only we
> disciples will see you and
> your love? What about
> everyone else?**

> **I and my Father will
> show ourselves to the
> world through you and
> other Christians loving me
> and obeying me!**

Wow!

People see what Jesus is like when
they see Christians living for Him
and obeying Him! We should be a
picture of Jesus to those around us!

Action!

How can you be a picture of Jesus
to people around you?

_____
_____
_____
_____
_____
_____
_____

Ask God to help you.

**John
14 v 25-31**

Imagine that you're going to leave your family forever and go to live in Outer Mongolia.

What would you give your family as a parting present?

_____
_____
_____
_____
_____
_____
_____

WEIRD WORDS

Advocate
Helper

Prince of this world
Satan, the devil

Present day

Jesus is going to leave His disciples with **two amazing presents**.

Read John 14 v 25-26

... and go backwards one letter.

1. _ _ _ _
I P M Z

_ _ _ _ _ _
T Q J S J U

Jesus would send the Holy Spirit to teach His followers (all Christians) how to live for God. And to remind them of Jesus' words to them.

Read verse 27

2. _ _   _ _ _ _ _
N Z   Q F B D F

Jesus would die on the cross to take the punishment for our sins. So we can be forgiven and be at peace with God!

And one day, God's people will live in real peace for ever!

Read verses 28-31

_ _ _   _ _ _ _ _
U I F   E F W J M

... has no power over Jesus (v30)! So how was Jesus killed by His enemies?

Jesus _ _ _ _ _
M P W F T
His Father and does what His Father

_ _ _ _ _ _ _ _
D P N N B O E T

It was **God's plan** that Jesus should die so that we can have our sins forgiven. Jesus loves His Father. So Jesus obeyed Him, willingly died and went to be with His Father.

And He wants the whole world to know it!

Pray!

Read through today's boxes again and thank God for the amazing gifts He's given us.
And ask God to help you tell the world why Jesus died.

That's vine by me!

**John
15 v 1-8**

*Quick quiz.
What's a vine?*

*a) German for
"wine"* ☐

*b) a strange
cat-like animal
with five
legs and
two tails* ☐

*c) a plant that
grapes
grow on* ☐

The answer is c!

WEIRD WORDS

Prunes
Cuts off the ends of
branches so they will
grow back better

Disciples
Jesus' followers, who
learn from Him

In the Old Testament, the Israelites (God's people) were often called **the vine**. But the Israelites kept disobeying God. They were like a vine that produced bad fruit.

Read John 15 v 1-3
Who is the true vine?

J_____

Jesus described Himself as the **true vine**. His followers (including you and me!) are the **branches**. That means we have a close relationship with Him.

> *What's wrong with one of the branches in the picture?*

There's no fruit. It's dead. Useless.

Who is the gardener (v1)?

God the F_____

People who don't bear fruit (don't live God's way) will be **cut off** from God (v2). But those who do serve Him, God will help to become even more fruitful (v2)!

Read verses 4-6
How does Jesus say we can avoid being cut off from God (v4)?

R_____ in me and

I will r_____

in y_____

Stay connected to Jesus! A branch can only produce grapes when it's connected to the vine.

So we can only serve God properly when we're connected to Jesus. When we're forgiven by Him, living for Him, learning from Him. We're useless without Jesus.

Read verses 7-8
We can ask God to help us serve Him. And He will!

Pray!

If you're a Christian, thank God that you're connected to Jesus. Then look at your list under Action! on day 47. Ask God to help you to serve Him in those ways. Then do it!

Friends united

**John
15 v 9-17**

Quickly write down some of your friends' names.

_____
_____
_____
_____
_____

How do you show someone that you're their friend?

_____
_____
_____
_____
_____

Are you Jesus' friend?

Yes ☐

No ☐

Not sure ☐

Read John 15 v 9-11

Fill in the vowels to show what it means to be a friend of Jesus.

1. Being l__v__d by J__s__s (v9)

2. K__ __p__ng J__s__s' c__mm__nds (v10)

3. Having j__y (v11)

If we love Jesus, we'll obey what He's said. We'll live for Him. And the great news is that friendship with Jesus will make us happy!

Read verses 12-14

What specific command should Jesus' friends obey (v12)?

L__v__ each __th__r as I have l__v__d y__ __

How did Jesus show His love for us (v13)?

H__ l__ __d d__wn H__s l__f__ f__r H__s fr__ __nds

Jesus was prepared to die for us, so that we could have our wrongs forgiven and live forever with Him! And He expects us to show love for others. To put others first.

Read verses 15-17

Wow! Jesus has told us how His Father God wants us to live (v15)! If you're a Christian, He chose **YOU** to live for Him (v16)! And you can ask God to help you live for Him (v16)!

One great way we can show that we are Jesus' friends is by showing love for each other (v17).

Think!

Do you show love for the people around you? In what ways can you put other people first?

_____
_____
_____
_____

**John
15 v 18-25**

*Jesus is still
telling us what it
means to be His
friend.*

*It makes quite
uncomfortable
reading...*

King of the hassle

In today's Bible bit, "**the world**" means people who don't live their lives for God. Now get ready for some fast facts...

Read John 15 v 18-21

Fact 1: Jesus ch_____ you! (v19)

If you're a Christian, Jesus chose you to be one of His friends!

Fact 2: Christians will be persecuted for being J_____ friend (v20)

People who don't live for Jesus don't love Him. So you can expect to get hassled by them. Teasing, name-calling, sometimes worse.

Fact 3: People p_____d Jesus too (v20)

Jesus was taunted, tortured and killed. He went through far more than we ever will. So He understands the hassles we go through! We can talk to Him honestly and openly about them.

Read verses 22-25

Fact 4: There is no excuse for rejecting J_____

People who met Jesus heard His words. They saw His amazing miracles. They had no excuse for rejecting Him and refusing to live for God.

We've read Jesus' words in the Bible. We've seen people's lives changed by Him. We have no excuse for ignoring Him and continuing to sin against Him.

Pray!

Who do you know who rejects Jesus? Ask God to use you to talk to them about Jesus.

Pray again!

If you get hassled for being a Christian, thank Jesus that He understands what you're going through. Ask Him to give you the strength (and courage) to face it for Him.

WEIRD WORDS

Persecuted
Attacked, treated unfairly

The one
God the Father

Fulfil
Make come true

Law
Old Testament

Holy Helper

**John
15 v 26 – 16 v 4**

*Jesus says
His friends
(Christians)
can expect to
be hassled for
following Him.*

*But we're not
on our own!*

WEIRD WORDS

**Advocate/
Spirit of truth**
The Holy Spirit

Testify
Tell people about
Jesus

Synagogue
Where people met
to learn from the
Old Testament. To
be banned from
going was terrible.

Read John 15 v 26-27

*Who has Jesus sent to help us out
(v26)? Unscramble the anagrams.*

H_____ S_____

LYHO ISTRIP

*What does the Holy Spirit help us
to do?*

T_____ P_____

LETL PLOPEE

A_____ J_____

UBOAT SEJSU

The disciples had spent three years
with Jesus, so they had loads they
could tell people.

But we know Jesus too! We have
seen His effect on our lives. And we
know what the Bible tells us about
Him.

Think!

Who can YOU tell about Jesus?

_____

_____

_____

_____

Read John 16 v 1-4

*What would happen when the
disciples told people about Jesus?*

They'd be thrown out of the

S_____

USEANYGOG

or even K_____ (v2)

ILLDEK

Jesus warned them about this, so
they wouldn't give up (v1). And
when it came true, they'd realise
that Jesus had been telling the truth
(v4). They could trust Him to help
them. And so can we!

Pray!

Thank God for giving you the
Holy Spirit to help you tell people
about Jesus. Ask God to give you
opportunities to talk to the people
you wrote down earlier.

For the free e-booklet *How Do I show
I'm a Christian?*, email
discover@thegoodbook.co.uk
or check out
www.thegoodbook.co.uk/contact-us
to find our UK mailing address.

Exodus: God rules, OK?

**Exodus
25 v 1-9**

Read Exodus 24 v 15-18 for a reminder

Today we get back to Moses in Exodus. He's at the top of Mount Sinai with God!

Read Exodus 24 v 15-18 for a reminder

God has already given Moses the Ten Commandments to show the Israelites how to live for Him. Now God has some more instructions for them...

Read Exodus 25 v 1-7

Moses was to ask the people to give certain things to God. Find some of them in the wordsearch (they're in verses 3-7).

B	V	T	H	N	C	Q	E
L	S	P	I	C	E	S	R
M	I	O	Y	F	G	K	B
F	L	I	N	E	N	I	R
X	V	L	U	D	K	N	O
J	E	W	E	L	S	S	N
T	R	J	Z	P	B	A	Z
D	S	G	O	L	D	O	E

G_ _ _

S_ _ _ _ _

B_ _ _ _ _

FINE L_ _ _ _ _

RAMS' S_ _ _ _ _

O_ _

S_ _ _ _ _

J_ _ _ _ _

So what were all these special metals, jewels and materials for?

Read verses 8-9

The Israelites were on their way to Canaan, the land God had promised to give them. As they travelled, God would be with them all the time. So God ordered them to build a special tent (tabernacle) where God would be among them.

Action!

What can YOU give to God's work? Pocket money? Old toys for the toddlers' club?

_____

_____

Pray!

Thank God that He wants to be with His people all the time. Thank God that these days, His Holy Spirit is living in the lives of all Christians, so He's with them all the time!

WEIRD WORDS

Offering
Gift to God

Acacia
A spiky type of tree

Anointing oil
Oil poured on the heads of God's chosen servants

Fragrant incense
Powder burnt to make a sweet smell

Onyx
Precious stone

Ephod and breastplate
Special robes worn by a priest

Sanctuary/ Tabernacle
Special place set aside for God

Tents moment

**Exodus
25 v 10-22**

Yesterday we read how Moses was going to build a massive tent!

It would be called the tabernacle, where God would be with His people.

WEIRD WORDS

Ark
Wooden box

Cubit
About 50cm

Covenant law
Stones with Ten Commandments on them

Cherubim
Angel-like creatures

Read Exodus 25 v 10-15

The first thing to go inside the tabernacle would be a large wooden box called an **ark**. No, that's not the same as Noah's Ark! This was a wooden box. But it was no ordinary box...

Fill in the spaces using the verses you've just read.

moulding made of _____

poles of _____

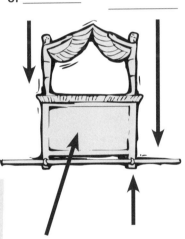

box covered with _____

_____ **rings**

Read verse 16

The two stone tablets, with the Ten Commandments written on them, were to go in the ark. God's instructions to the Israelites were so important, they were kept in a very special place.

Think!

Are God's words in the Bible special to you? Do you love to read them and learn them and obey them?

Read verses 17-22

They were to make a special cover for the box. God would meet with His people there to instruct them! The special cover was called the **atonement cover** (or mercy seat).

Atonement cover

Atonement means having your sins forgiven by God so that you can live with Him. The atonement cover was so-called because this box was a sign of the great **forgiveness** God showed the Israelites again and again.

Pray!

It may sound odd, but JESUS is our mercy seat. He's the one we go to for forgiveness. If we turn to Him, He will forgive us for all the wrong things we've done. Thank Jesus for making it possible for us to live with God!

Calf hearted

**Exodus
32 v 1-6**

*Moses is with God
on Mount Sinai.*

*He's been so long
that the people
don't think he's
coming back!*

WEIRD WORDS

Aaron
Moses' brother

Idol
Fake god

Altar
Table where gifts to
the idol were put

**Sacrificed burnt
offerings**
Gave gifts of cooked
meat

Revelry
Partying

Read Exodus 32 v 1-6

Cross out the wrong answers.

**When Moses had been gone
a long time, the people
turned to Joshua/Aaron/
Hairyone (v1). They asked
him to make gods/goats for
them to worship (v1).
Aaron told them to bring
him their gold/silver/plastic
earrings (v2).
The people gave Aaron their
gold bracelets/earrings/hair
clips (v3). He melted the gold
and made a statue shaped
like a calf/foal/duckling (v4).
The people said, "This is the
god who rescued us from
Israel/Egypt/Ebay (v4)!"
They held a carnival/festival/
circus for the gold calf (v5)
and offered it socks/sacks/
sacrifices (v6).**

How quickly they forgot all the
amazing things God had done for
them! They even pretended that this
golden calf had rescued them!

*What had they promised God 40
days earlier? (Flick back to **Exodus
24 v 3** and fill in the speech bubble.)*

> **We will do**
> e_____
> **the Lord has said**

It wasn't long before they turned
away from God. Are you shocked by
what the Israelites did? As we read
more of Exodus, we'll see that they
often forgot what God had done for
them, and stopped trusting Him and
living His way.

Sadly, **we're like that too**. We can
easily forget God and turn away
from Him, living our way instead of
living to please Him.

Pray!

*Dear God, I'm sorry for the times
I've turned away from You. Please
help me never to forget all you've
done for me. Please help me to
keep trusting you, no matter how
hard that is. Amen.*

58

Exodus 32 v 7-14

Pain in the neck

The Israelites had turned away from God. They got Aaron to build a gold statue of a calf and they worshipped that instead of God!

Read Exodus 32 v 7-10

What did God call the people (v9)?

St_____

God had shown them the **best way** to live. But they were like stubborn donkeys that only go the way they want to. They refused to live God's way and went their **own way** instead. So God called them **stiff-necked**!

The Israelites had turned away from God and deserved to be punished. God was going to destroy them and start a new nation from Moses' family (v10).

Read verses 11-14

Use the backwards word pool to complete what Moses said.

caasl   esimorp

snaitpygE   stnavres

llik   sniatnuom

**Why should the
E_____ say:
"You brought your
people out of Egypt to
k_____ them in the
m_____."
Remember your p_____
to your s_____
Abraham, I_____
and Israel (Jacob).**

Did God destroy the Israelites (v14)?

Yes/No _____

The Israelites had sinned. They **deserved** to die. But instead, God showed them **mercy** — that's **undeserved** kindness. We'll find out more about sin, anger and mercy tomorrow.

Pray!

Thank God that He is merciful — showing loving kindness to all His people (including you and me!) when we deserve the opposite.

WEIRD WORDS

Corrupt
Sinful

Sacrificed
Gave gifts of food

Stiff-necked/ Stubborn
Refusing to live God's way

Evil intent
Determined to do evil

Relent
Let them off and forgive them

Numerous
Many

Inheritance
The Israelites were God's people and would receive the land He promised them

Dealing with sin

**Exodus
32 v 15-35**

*The Israelites
are in serious
trouble...*

They had sinned against God by
making and worshipping a gold calf.
They turned away from God and put
a useless statue in His place! Moses
was furious...

Read Exodus 32 v 15-24

*What did Moses do to the stones
with the Ten Commandments on
them (v19)?*

Wow!

That's true for us too. We all sin
— and sin **must** be punished. The
great news is that someone came to
take the punishment in our place!

*What did Moses do to the gold calf
(v20)?*

- B_____ it in the fire
- Ground it into p_____
- M_____ it with water
- Made the Israelites
  d_____ it

*Moses wanted the people to realise
the seriousness of turning away
from God.*

When Jesus was nailed to the cross,
He took all our sin onto Himself,
taking the punishment we deserve.
He died in our place. Anyone who
trusts Jesus' death to rescue them
from God's punishment is forgiven
by God!

WEIRD WORDS

Covenant Law
Stones with Ten
Commandments
written on them

**Inscribed/
Engraved**
Had writing on

Joshua
Moses' assistant

Prone to evil
Always seem to do
wrong

Levites
Tabernacle workers

Atonement
Ask God to forgive
them

Read verses 25-35

Depressing stuff, but God was
totally fair. The Israelites had
sinned, and sin must always be
punished. Some of them were
killed because of what they had
done (v28), and others became ill
(v35). God couldn't let their sin go
unpunished.

Pray!

Thank God for loving you so
much that He sent His own Son,
Jesus, to die for you.

For the free e-booklet
Why did Jesus die?, email
discover@thegoodbook.co.uk
or check out
www.thegoodbook.co.uk/contact-us
to find our UK mailing address.

With or without God?

Exodus 33 v 1-11

The Israelites had worshipped statues instead of God.

The Lord was not pleased...

WEIRD WORDS

Oath
Very serious promise

Descendants
People who would be born into their family

Mourn
Be very upset and sad

Ornaments
Gold and silver jewellery

Read Exodus 33 v 1-3

That's amazing! Even though they had turned away from God, He would still give them the land He had promised them! He would send an angel to drive their enemies out of that land (v2).

Wow!

God gives His people so much more than they deserve. We deserve to be punished for our sin, but God sent Jesus to rescue us. And He continues to give His people (Christians) so many good things!

However, God had some bad news for the Israelites too (v3).

*Find it by writing out the **CAPITAL LETTERS**.*

imiIWghtdILeLN
strOToyyoGOuWonI
THtheYOwUay

— — — — — — — —

— — — — — — — — —

Think!

Would that have bothered you? Are you happy to carry on doing things your own way, without God? Or do you want to be one of God's people, living His way, with Him in charge of your life?

Why wouldn't God go with them? (Use the smaller letters.)

Read verses 4-6

The Israelites were sorry for what they had done. Maybe there was still hope for them.

Read verses 7-11

God was Moses' friend and listened to what Moses said. Tomorrow we'll see Moses pleading with God to go with them.

Pray!

Thank God that He is always with His people. Jesus has made it possible for us to talk to Him any time at all!

61

**Exodus
33 v 11-17**

God said He
wouldn't be
with His people
because they had
been disobedient.

They had built
a statue and
worshipped it
instead of God.

But was God
angry with Moses
too?

Powerful prayer!

Read Exodus 33 v 11-12

Moses hadn't disobeyed God. Verses 11-12 say some very special things about what God thought of Moses. *Use the code to find them.*

**1. God spoke with Moses
face to face, as a man**

(v11)

2. God said

(v12)

3.

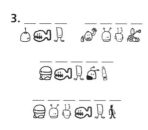

God had already answered one of Moses' prayers.

PRAYER ANSWER 1

The Israelites wouldn't be destroyed. They could still go to the land God promised to give them.

But Moses wasn't satisfied!

He needed God to go with them. How would God answer Moses this time?

Read verses 13-17

… and fill in God's answer (v14).

> **PRAYER ANSWER 2**

Amazing! God loves to answer prayers like that! Do you want Him to answer yours? Then follow Moses' great example…

Pray!

- Spend a lot of time talking with God.
- Pray for things which will honour God, not yourself.
- Never give up praying!
- When God answers one prayer, don't stop, keep praying about other things!

A	B	D	E	F	H	I	K	M	N	O	P	R	S	T	U	V	W	Y

What's God really like?

Exodus 33 v 18-23

Moses is talking with God.

And he's about to ask God for something very special.

WEIRD WORDS

Proclaim
Tell everyone

Mercy
Undeserved kindness

Compassion
Loving kindness

Cleft
Dent or hole in the rock

Glory
Impressiveness

What kind of things do **you** *ask God for? Fill in the speech bubble with some answers.*

I bet you don't ask God for the same thing that Moses did...

Read Exodus 33 v 18

... and fill in what he said.

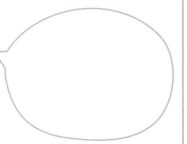

Think!

Do you want the same thing? For God to show you what He's like? How great and powerful and loving He is? That's what God's glory is.

Read verses 19-23

That was an even better answer than Moses expected. Moses asked to **see** God's glory (v18).

But God was going to let Moses **hear** his name (v19).

In other words, He'd make Moses understand what God is really like.

Moses saw how God is full of **goodness, mercy** and **compassion**.

Wow!

Only in eternity will God's people be able to see the full glory of God. Even Moses was only allowed to see just a little of what God's like. But we can get to know God better and find out what He's like by reading His book, the Bible.

Pray!

As you read about God in the Bible, ask Him to help you understand more of how great and powerful and loving He really is.

Love from above

**Exodus
34 v 1-8**

*Moses is going
back up the
mountain to
meet God
again.*

WEIRD WORDS

Chisel
Carve out

Tablets
Slabs of stone

Compassionate
Full of love and
kindness

Gracious
Giving people far
more than they
deserve

Abounding
Full of

Faithfulness
Completely
trustworthy

Maintaining
Keeping up

Rebellion
Disobeying God

Read Exodus 34 v 1-4

Moses had smashed the stones with
the Ten Commandments on them.
So he took two new stones for God
to write on.

Yesterday we read that Moses asked
God to show him what He's really
like...

Read verses 5-7

Fill in what Moses learned.

1. What God is like (v6)
C__mp__ss__ __nate
Gr__cious
Slow to ang__r

Do you ever feel that people don't
fully understand you? Or they soon
get impatient with you? God is the
opposite of that! He loves us and is
so patient with us.

2. What God is full of (v6)
Abounding in l__v__
and f__ __thf__ln__ss

God will never let you down.
There is no limit to His love and
faithfulness.

3. What God shows to
people (v7)
Maintaining l__v__
to th__ __s__nds

God has a special love for ALL His
children — Christians. Do you think
there's room for you too?

4. What God will forgive (v7)
W__ck__dn__ss and
r__bellion and s__n

Do you seem to have so many
faults that you feel God couldn't
possibly forgive you? IT'S NOT TRUE!
God loves to forgive our wrongs,
however big they are.

That's the best kind of love to find
out about — **God's incredible love
for you!**

Read verse 8

Pray!

Like Moses, praise and thank God
for His amazing love.

Put God first

Exodus 34 v 8-14

The Israelites had disobeyed God. So God said He would not be with them as they travelled.

WEIRD WORDS

Stiff-necked
Stubborn, sinful

Covenant
Agreement between God and the Israelites

Treaty
Peace agreement

Snare
Trap

Sacred stones/ Asherah poles
Used in worshipping fake gods

Jealous
God hates idol worship

Read Exodus 34 v 8-9

Moses knew that the Israelites needed God with them. He asked God to take them as His inheritance — **His special people**.

Read verses 10-11

Despite their sin, God would be with His people! *What did God say (v10)? Take **every third letter**, beginning with the **first I**.*

I I D M W O M I N A L O K L
T I D W N R O G I R A V S C E
H O O I V U P E T A N Y N A O
Y N U O T R T W E H I N E T
E R H M G Y I O O E D U S S

I '_ _ _ _ _ _ _

_ _ _ _ _ _ _ _ _

_ _ _ _ _ _ _ _

God made a special covenant agreement with His people.

*What was God's side of it? Take every third letter, beginning with the **second I**.*

I _ _ _ _ _ _ _ _ _

_ _ _ _ _ _ _

_ _ _ _ _ _

God promised to give the Israelites the land of Canaan to live in. And He promised to drive out the sinful people who lived there (v11).

Read verses 12-14

What was the Israelites' part of the covenant? Take every third letter, beginning with **D**.

D_ _ _ _ _

_ _ _ _ _ _ _

_ _ _ _ _ _ _ _

_ _ _ _

God told them to have nothing to do with the other nations and their evil ways. They must destroy their fake gods and not worship them.

God hates it when we worship anything other than Him. He demands that we put Him **first** in our lives. There should be **nothing** more important to us than God.

Think!

What things can sometimes be more important to you than God?

_____

_____

_____

Pray!

Ask God to help you put Him first in your life, so that you serve Him and nothing else.

God rules, ok

**Exodus
34 v 15-28**

God had loads of extra instructions for the Israelites...

1. Don't be led astray
Read Exodus 34 v 15-17

God told His people to have nothing to do with other nations. These people worshipped false gods. If the Israelites became friends with them, they would end up worshipping these fake gods too.

Action!

Is there anyone you hang out with who persuades you to do wrong? Pleasing God and obeying Him must be more important to us than pleasing our friends. Maybe you need to stay away from that person.

2. Celebrate the festival of unleavened bread
Read verse 18

They celebrated this feast to remember God rescuing them from Egypt.

Action!

How can you remember what God has done for you? Maybe you could write a diary, keeping a note of what God has done in your life, prayers He's answered, etc.

3. Give God the best!
Read verses 19-20

They were to give the best of their animals to God as a sign of their devotion to Him.

Action!

What can you give to God? Pocket money? More of your time, helping out at church?

Verses 21-28 have more instructions about the Sabbath rest day and other festivals. We're not expected to keep all the same rules as the Israelites — they were specially for the Israelites, not us. But we can still learn from some of these rules. Read through the Action! points again and decide what you most need to do.

Pray!

Have you decided? Ask God to help you do it. Ask Him to help you devote your life to living His way.

WEIRD WORDS

Prostitute themselves
Serve fake gods

Sacrifice
Offer gifts of food

Unleavened
Made without yeast

Yeast
Stuff used to make bread rise

Offspring
Babies

Livestock
Animals

Redeem
Buy back

Firstfruits
First crops

Sovereign
In control of everything

**Exodus
34 v 29-35**

*On Mount Sinai,
God has been
giving Moses
instructions
for how the
Israelites should
live.*

*Now Moses
goes back down
the mountain to
tell the people
what God has
said.*

WEIRD WORDS

**Tablets of the
covenant law**
Stones with Ten
Commandments on
them

Radiant
Shining

Veil
Cloth hanging over
his face

Ready steady glow

Read Exodus 34 v 29-32

Cross out the wrong answers!

**Moses came down from
Mount Sinus/Sinai, carrying
the terrapin/television/ten
commandments (v29). His
face was radiant and shining
because he had washed/
shaved/spoken with the Lord
(v29). When Amos/Aaron/
Ainsley and the people saw
Moses, they were afraid/
amused/amazed (v30). But
Mooses/Moses called them
together and spoke to them
(v31). Moses gave them all
the sweets/commands the
Lord had given him (v32).**

Because Moses had been with God,
his face was shining! Spending time
with God has an amazing effect on
people!

Read verses 33-35

**When Moses finished
speaking to them, he put a
vole/veil over his face/feet/
bellybutton (v33). Whenever
Moses went into God's
presents/presence in the
tent, he burned/removed/
washed the veil (v34). Each
time Moses met with God, he
told the Iranians/Israelites/
voles what God had
said (v34).**

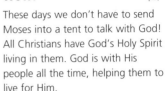

Wow!

These days we don't have to send
Moses into a tent to talk with God!
All Christians have God's Holy Spirit
living in them. God is with His
people all the time, helping them to
live for Him.

And we don't have shining faces,
but other people should be able
to tell we're God's people by the
things we do and say.

Action!

What do you need to change in
your life so that people can tell that
you live for God?

_____

_____

_____

Pray!

Thank God that He is always with
His people. Ask Him to help you
get stuck into doing what you've
written down.

Guide and seek

**Exodus
40 v 34-38**

Chapters 35 – 40 of Exodus are about setting up the tabernacle — the tent where God was with His people.

Now we jump to the end of Exodus...

WEIRD WORDS

Tent of meeting/ Tabernacle
A special, huge tent where God was among His people. It reminded the Israelites that God was with them all the time.

Read Exodus 40 v 34-38

What covered the tent of meeting (v34)?

A pillar of fire ☐

A cloud ☐

A clown ☐

When the cloud was over the tent, God's glory filled it. ·

When that happened, what couldn't Moses do (v35)?

Eat bread with yeast ☐

Go up the mountain ☐

Enter the tent ☐

When could the Israelites move on (v36)?

When the cloud was there ☐

When the cloud lifted ☐

When Moses said so ☐

Wow!

They only moved on when the Lord's cloud lifted. God was guiding them all the time. God guides His people. We have the Bible to show us how to live. And we can ask God to help us make wise decisions.

What could the Israelites see at all times (v38)?

Moses' shining face ☐

Mount Sinai ☐

The cloud of the Lord ☐

Wow!

The powerful, awesome God, who created the whole world, was living with His people! They knew He was with them at all times.

Christians today have God's Holy Spirit living in them. God is with them always, guiding them!

Pray!

Thank God that His people can be confident that He is with them. Ask God to guide you through life, so that you live the way He wants you to.

Revelation: Jesus revealed

**Revelation
12 v 1-6**

Back to the book of Revelation, where John is telling us what he saw in an awesome vision.

It reveals the truth about JESUS, and the perfect plan to rescue people from sin.

Before we jump into today's Bible bit, we need to know what some of the things in it mean. *Follow the trails to find out what means what.*

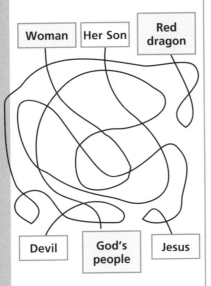

Woman | Her Son | **Red dragon**

Devil | **God's people** | Jesus

Remember these meanings as you read today's Bible bit.

Read Revelation 12 v 1-4

Jesus (the son) was going to be born as a human baby. But the devil (dragon) was waiting, and wanted to destroy Jesus.

Read verse 5

The son was born. Before the dragon could destroy him, he was taken up to be with God.

Wow. That's a double-quick version of Jesus' life! Complete it by filling in the missing vowels.

**He was b__rn as a h__m__n
b__by. When he gr__w up,
people k__ll__d Him on the
cr__ss. But he b__ __t
d__ __th, came b__ck to l__fe
and then went to h__ __ven
to rule with His F__th__r!**

The devil failed! But while Jesus is in heaven, what happens to His people (Christians) on earth?

Read verse 6

This is saying that God's people (the woman) are safe from the devil (the dragon)! Even though the devil tries to get at them, God keeps them safe!

Pray!

Praise God that the devil has failed! And that God protects His people from the devil!

**Revelation
12 v 7-17**

Dragon's den

*For today's answers, go backwards
one letter.*

*In today's bit of
John's vision, the
red dragon is
trying to kill the
woman.*

*It's all about how
the devil (the
dragon) attacks
God's people (the
woman).*

Read Revelation 12 v 7-9

The devil (Satan) used to be an
angel in heaven. But he got thrown
out for going against God. *So what
does he do now? (v9)*

M F B E T   U I F

X P S M E

B T U S B Z

The devil tries to tempt people to go
against God.

Read verses 10-12

*What does the devil do to Christians
(v10)?*

B D D V T F T

U I F N

P G   T J O

*But how do Christians beat the devil
(v11)?*

1. _ _ _   _ _ _ _ _
U I F   C M P P E

_ _   _ _ _
P G   U I F

_ _ _ _
M B N C

Earlier in Revelation, we discovered
that the Lamb is Jesus. He died on
the cross and came back to life to
beat the devil for us!

2. _ _ _   _ _ _ _
U I F   X P S E

_ _   _ _ _ _ _
P G   U I F J S

_ _ _ _ _ _ _ _
U F T U J N P O Z

This means living for God and
obeying His Word (the Bible). If we
do this, we can stand up against the
devil!

Read verses 13-17

This tells us that the devil is furious
and will constantly attack Christians.
But God protects His people from
the devil.

Pray!

Ask God to help you obey Him
and stand up against the devil's
attacks. Thank God that He has
promised to keep us safe from
the devil!

Dragging the dragon

Revelation 20 v 1-10

Let's jump forward to chapter 20.

The dragon (the devil) is still attacking God's people (Christians).

WEIRD WORDS

Abyss
Very deep pit

Testimony
Evidence

Blessed and holy / Priests
Set apart to serve God

Resurrection
Coming back to life

Second death
Hell

Breadth
All of it

Read Revelation 20 v 1-3

Use the word pool to fill in the gaps.

> 1000   Christians
> Satan   ever   victory
> Abyss   throw   Jesus
> devil   people

The d_____ is thrown into the A_____ where he is chained for _____ years.

This doesn't mean exactly 1000 years. It's talking about the time in between Jesus' resurrection and when He comes back to earth. That's right now!

Right now, the devil is in chains. God is stopping him from ruling the world. He still tempts us and turns people against God, but he's **NOT IN CHARGE**.

He can't stop people hearing about Jesus!

Read verses 4-6

J_____ beat sin and the devil when He died and rose again. He's in charge. So all His followers, C_____, rule with Him. It's their v_____ too!

Read verses 7-10

But S_____ (the devil) will be set free and will attempt one last attack on God's p_____.
Then Jesus will t_____ the devil into hell to be punished for e_____.

The devil is powerful. Watch out for his attacks. But Jesus has already beaten him, and he will be punished in hell for ever!

Pray!

Think of specific ways the devil attacks you. Ask God to help you not to give in to the devil's temptations.

For the free e-booklet *Why did Jesus rise?*, email discover@thegoodbook.co.uk or check out www.thegoodbook.co.uk/contact-us to find our UK mailing address.

71

In the good books?

**Revelation
20 v 11-15**

God has defeated
the devil, who
will be thrown
into hell for ever.

But he's not the
only one who will
have to face God.

One day everyone
will have to stand
before God's
throne...

Read Revelation 20 v 11-14

Imagine the awesome scene...

> Everyone who has ever
> lived is gathered before God's
> throne. Kings and beggars,
> cavemen and pop stars.
> People from every kind of
> background, from every nation.
> Me and you too. We all stand
> speechless at the awesome God
> who sits on the throne. Then the
> huge books are slowly opened...

> **What are these
> books all about?**

> **They're a record of
> everything everyone's
> ever done in their life.**

> **If God knows every
> bad thing we've done,
> surely there's no chance
> of getting to heaven!**

> **Ah, but there's
> another book...**

Read verse 15

Everyone who has trusted Jesus to
forgive their sins has their name in
the **book of life**. They will live with
Him for ever! Everyone else will be
punished in hell (the lake of fire).

Pray!

Thank God that Christians will
one day go to live with Him,
despite all the wrong things
they've done!

WEIRD WORDS

Hades
Hell

Think!

What things from your life wouldn't
you want anyone to read about?

_____

_____

_____

Still not sure if that includes you?
For info on how to become a
Christian email
discover@thegoodbook.co.uk
or check out
www.thegoodbook.co.uk/contact-us
to find our UK mailing address.

For heaven's sake

Revelation 21 v 1-8

NO MORE!

We're at the end of the world.

The devil (and everyone who has turned against God) will be thrown into hell.

What about everyone who's left?

WEIRD WORDS

Dwelling-place
His home

Mourning
Being upset and distressed

Idolators
People who worshipped false gods

Read Revelation 21 v 1-4

How awesome does that sound?! Christians won't go to heaven — heaven will come to them! Actually it will be a new earth to live in (v1)!

*Now blast away the **X**s to find the best part (v3).*

XXGOXXDWXILXLXLI
XXVEXWIXXTHXHXISXPEX
OPXLXXEFXXORXEVXXERX

— — — — — — —

— — — —

— — — — — — —

— — — — — — — —

— — — — — — —

What else (v4)?

NOXMOXXREXDEXX
ATHMOXXURNIXNGCRYX
XXIXNGOXXRXPAXIXNX

— — — — — —

— — — — —

— — — — — — —

— — — — — —

Read verses 5-6

Alpha and Omega are A and Z in Greek. God is the first and the last: **He is the God of all time and history!**

To those who live for God, He gives **eternal life** with Him (that's what v6 means).

Read verses 7-8

God has told us about the amazing new heaven and earth that He will create. *What does He say will happen to those who stick at living for Him?*

XTHEXXYXWIXLXLIXN
HEXXRIXTAXLXLTHIXSXX

— — — — — — —

— — — — — — —

— — — — — — —

More about that tomorrow. But those who turn away from God will be thrown into hell (v8).

Pray!

Who do you know who doesn't live for God (maybe yourself)? Ask God to save them, so they can serve Him and live with Him for ever.

Look on the bride side

Revelation 21 v 9-14

John has been telling us some amazing things.

And he's not finished yet...

All of today's answers can be found in the wordsearch.

C	U	D	Q	T	O	G	O	D
H	O	L	Y	Z	L	W	B	F
R	B	A	F	G	C	I	T	Y
I	C	M	J	L	Y	F	E	O
S	K	B	R	I	D	E	N	R
T	P	U	E	R	J	T	U	G
I	C	V	B	N	E	A	N	L
A	H	P	L	S	S	O	K	O
N	A	G	H	C	U	L	S	R
S	H	I	N	E	S	D	L	Y

Read Revelation 21 v 9

What is the angel going to show John?

The B_____, the

W_____ of

the L_____

The Lamb is J_____. So the bride of the Lamb means God's people, C_____!

Read verses 10-14

Instead of seeing a bride, John saw the

H_____ C_____

The **Holy City** is a picture of God's people living with Him for ever. All of God's people who have ever lived will be there!

How is the Holy City described in verse 11?

It S_____ with

the G_____

of G_____

Wow!

Life right now may seem great. Or it may be a real pain. But if you're one of God's people, you can look forward to eternal life with Him. It will be amazing!

Pray!

God's people (Christians) will shine with God's glory! They will show how great, wonderful and perfect God is. Thank God for this fantastic privilege.

WEIRD WORDS

Lamb
Jesus Christ

Jasper
Precious jewel

Twelve apostles
Jesus' twelve disciples

Revelation 21 v 12-21

John is seeing a vision of the Holy City — a picture of Christians living for ever with God!

WEIRD WORDS

12,000 stadia
2200 kilometres

144 cubits
65 metres

Agate, onyx, chrysolite, beryl, topaz, turquoise, jacinth, amethyst
Precious jewels

City limits

Read Revelation 21 v 12-14

Time to do some number-crunching!

There were _____ gates with the names of the

_____

of Israel on them.

There were _____ foundations with the names of the _____

_____ of

the Lamb (Jesus).

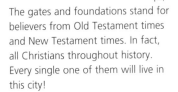

Wow!

The gates and foundations stand for believers from Old Testament times and New Testament times. In fact, all Christians throughout history. Every single one of them will live in this city!

But will they be safe there?

Read verses 15-17

The city is

_____

long, wide and high.

The wall is

_____

thick/high.

This shows us that God's people will be **totally safe** with Him. No one will be able to attack them any more!

*Look up **Psalm 125 v 2** and fill in the missing words.*

As the _____

surround _____,

so the _____ surrounds

His _____ both now

and for _____

Read that through again — it's so encouraging!

Read Revelation 21 v 18-21

It will be a beautiful place. It will be **perfect**.

Pray!

All Christians will live together with God! They will be safe with Him for ever! Want to say a big thank you?

75

Revelation 21 v 22-27

Something is missing from this picture.

No prizes for guessing what it is.

And it's not the only thing missing today.

WEIRD WORDS

Splendour
Riches, wealth

Deceitful
Deceiving

Lamb's book of life
Book which contains the names of everyone whose sin has been forgiven by Jesus

Bright lights, big city

John is still telling us about the Holy City — Christians living with God. But some things seem to be missing...

Read Revelation 21 v 22

No t_ _ _ _ _ _

There will be no need for a special place to worship God because Christians won't be separated from Him. God the Father and His Son Jesus will be there with all believers!

Read verses 23-24

No s_ _ or m_ _n

The glory of God will be far brighter than any light, even the sun! The **light** also means things like truth, goodness and freedom from sin. All of these things come from God. His light shows His people how He wants them to live.

Read verses 25-26

G_ _ _ _ never shut
No n_ _ _t

There will be no darkness or danger or sin! Heaven will always be light and God's people will always be safe there. In fact, there's no need to shut the gates at all. Here's why...

Read verse 27

Nothing im_ _ _ _

Nothing sinful and no one who has rejected God will be able to enter. God cannot bear sin. Only people who have had their sins forgiven can be near to God.

Think & pray!

Only people whose names are in the book of life will be there. That means only people who have had their sins wiped out by Jesus. Does that include YOU? Talk to God about your answer right now.

We're now in the last chapter of the last book of the Bible, Revelation.

We're reading about what eternal life will be like for God's people.

Curse reverse

To get our heads around it, we need to dip into the first book of the Bible...

Read Genesis 3 v 1-7, 22-24

Adam and Eve disobeyed God. So all humans were **cursed**. They were banned from eating from the **tree of life** and from living for ever with God.

Now read Revelation 22 v 1-3

What did the angel show John? Fill in the missing vowels.

Th__ r__v__r __f th__ w__t__r __f l__f__ __nd th__ tr__ __ __f l__f__

And what's the great news?

There will no longer be any c__rs__ (v3)

Wow!

God will remove His curse. His people will be allowed to live for ever with Him! There will be no more pain or suffering (v2).

Read verses 3-5

What four great things do we learn about God's people?

1. They will w__rsh__p __nd s__rv__ H__m (v3)

2. They will s__ __ H__s f__c__ (v4)
Nothing will separate God from His people.

3. H__s n__m__ w__ll b__ __n th__ __r f__r__h__ __ds (v4)
They will belong completely to God.

4. They will r__ __gn f__r __v__r __nd __v__r (v5)
They're God's servants, but they'll rule with Him!

Pray!

Read through all those things again, and spend time praising and thanking God for these fantastic facts.

77

Angelic advice

Revelation 22 v 6-9

John's awesome vision is over.

Read Revelation 22 v 6

What does the angel say about John's vision?

In Revelation we've read loads about Jesus and how we need to turn to Him and turn away from sin. But it's not just a vision, it's the truth. Do you believe it?

Read verse 7

What does Jesus say?

Jesus is coming soon to judge the world. People who obey Him and trust Him for forgiveness are BLESSED. He is pleased with them. They will live with Him for ever.

Read verses 8-9

John tried to worship the angel. But the angel told him to worship God!

We must worship God throughout our everyday lives. That means obeying Him, serving Him and living for Him.

Pray!

Ask God to help you serve and obey Him more and more.

WEIRD WORDS

The God who inspires the prophets
God sent His Holy Spirit to help the prophets (God's messengers) tell people God's message

Blessed
God is pleased with them and gives them great things

Prophecy
God's message to people — what He's telling us in Revelation

A B C D E F G H I K L M N O P R S T U W Y

78

Inside or out?

*Today's verses
are tricky.*

*Use the word
pool to help
you fill in the
explanations.*

WEIRD WORDS

Prophecy
God's message to
people

Vile
Disgusting

Holy
Set apart to serve
God

Immoral
Disobeying God

Idolaters
Worshippers of fake
gods

Falsehood
Lying

---

soon   right   outside
disobey   Revelation   City
punish   now   reward   time
wrong   God   washed

Read Revelation 22 v 10

Jesus says don't ignore
the message of
R_____,
because it's important right
n_____. The t_____ is
near when Jesus will return
to judge the world.

Read verse 11

Even though Jesus could
return at any time,
people carry on with life
as normal. Those who
disobey God, continue to do
w_____. People who
live for God, continue to do
r_____.

Read verses 12-13

Again Jesus warns us that
He's coming s_____.
He will r_____ those
who have lived for Him,
but will p_____
everyone who has disobeyed
Him (v12). He can do this
because He is G_____ of all
time and history (v13)!

Jesus says there are two different
types of people.

Read verse 14

Some people have had their
sins w_____ away
by Jesus. They can enter the
Holy C_____ and live
for ever with Him!

Read verse 15

The rest continue to
d_____ Jesus.
They will have to stay
o_____ the city.
They will be punished
for ever.

Think!

Have you had your wrongs
forgiven by Jesus? Will you live
with Him for ever?
Not sure? Make certain you talk
to an older Christian about it. It's
hugely important!

79

Revelation 22 v 16-21

What a comeback!

Has anyone really famous ever visited your school or town?

_____

_____

_____

A visit like that needs loads of preparation to make sure it all goes to plan. There's usually lots of excitement too.

But one day there will be a far bigger event than a celeb visiting your school!

Read Revelation 22 v 16-17

What's the massive event?

J_____

coming back (v16)!

Who are crying out for Him to come back (v17)?

The S_____ and the

b_____ (v17)

The **bride** means all of God's people — Christians everywhere. They have the **Holy Spirit** helping them to live for God.

So they should be **longing for Jesus to come back**, to live with them forever!

Read verse 17 again

Whoever wants it, can

have the w_____ of

l_____.

That means **anyone** can turn to Jesus and have their wrongs forgiven by Him. They can live for ever with Him!

Read verses 18-19

Don't a_____ to or

t_____ away anything

from God's message in

Revelation.

God's Word is **PERFECT** — not to be added to or taken from!

Read verses 20-21

Remember, Jesus is coming soon! Are you excited?

Pray!

Tell Jesus how you feel about Him coming back, and why you feel like that. Be honest.
Then ask Him to get you excited about living with Him for ever. And ask Him to help you serve Him until He does come back.

WEIRD WORDS

Testimony
Evidence

Root and Offspring of David
Jesus was from the same family as King David

Morning star
Old Testament name for the King who would come to rescue God's people. That's Jesus!

Water of life/ Tree of life/ Holy city
Eternal life

Grace
Undeserved gift of forgiveness

Jesus: Unbeatable love

**John
16 v 5-11**

*Let's get back to
the last supper.*

We're throwing ourselves back into the book of **John**. Remember, Jesus is talking to His disciples on the night before His death.

The disciples were so sad at the thought of Jesus leaving them that they hadn't realised it would be...

1. Better for Jesus
Read John 16 v 5-6

They hadn't really shown much interest in where Jesus was going. They hadn't been glad for Him that He was going back to His Father, because they were feeling sorry for themselves.

2. Better for them!
Read verse 7

It was for their good that Jesus should go. His death would mean that their sins could be forgiven. And He would send the Holy Spirit to help them live for God.

The Holy Spirit (Advocate, Helper) would also have a deadly serious message for the world.

Read verses 8-11
... and fill in the missing words.

The Holy Spirit lets people know they are IN THE WRONG (guilty).

A. Wrong because of all their s_____ (v9)

Rejecting Jesus.

B. Wrong because of Jesus' ri_____ss (v10)

For thinking they are OK when they're not, compared to Jesus!

C. The world is in the wrong, which brings j_____ (v11)

The devil will be judged and punished by God. And so will everyone who rejects Jesus.

Pray!

1. Pray for the people you know who reject Jesus. Ask God to change their hearts so that Jesus rules their lives.

2. And thank the Lord for sending the Holy Spirit to be with Christians, helping them to live for God.

WEIRD WORDS

Grief
Great sadness

Advocate
Holy Spirit

Righteousness
Being right with God

Prince of this world
Satan, the devil

Condemned
Found guilty, to be punished

That's the Spirit!

**John
16 v 12-15**

*We're still in the
upstairs room
on the night
of Jesus' last
meal with His
disciples.*

*And He's telling
them (and us!)
about the Holy
Spirit.*

Are you a bit baffled by the Holy
Spirit? Not quite sure about what
He does or how He does it? Good!
Because today we're discovering THE
TRUTH ABOUT THE HOLY SPIRIT...

Read John 16 v 12-15

*Then use the verses and the
word pool to reveal what the
Holy Spirit does.*

FUTURE

COME   WILL

YOU   GUIDE

• He will _____ you
  into all truth (v13)

• He _____ speak what
  He hears from the Father
  (v13)

• He will tell you about
  things to _____ in the
  _____ (v13)

• He will take the things to
  do with Jesus and show
  them to _____ (v14)

All Christians have the Holy Spirit
with them! The Holy Spirit helps us
to understand what **Jesus** has done
for us. *To sum up all of these things,
fit the words from the word pool
into the grid.*

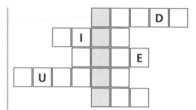

The Holy Spirit came to bring

to Jesus

Read verse 14 again

Wow!
The Holy Spirit helps us to
understand that Jesus died so our
sins can be forgiven.

He brings glory to Jesus — we
see how awesome and wonderful
Jesus is!

Pray!

Ask God for His Holy Spirit to
guide you in understanding the
truth about Jesus.

WEIRD WORDS

Spirit of truth
The Holy Spirit,
who helps us to
understand the truth
about Jesus

82 Pain relief

John 16 v 16-22

Jesus is telling the disciples that He will leave them very soon.

But it's not all bad news!

And it's got something to do with babies!

If you ask your mum about giving birth to you, she'll tell you about the awful pain she had to go through. But when you finally popped into the world, her pain turned into happiness!

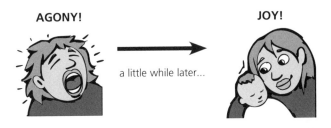

AGONY!   a little while later...   **JOY!**

Jesus was going to leave His disciples very soon. It was going to really hurt them. They would go through AGONY when He was taken away and killed. But it wouldn't last for long! "In a little while" they would be so thrilled that all the pain would be forgotten!

Read John 16 v 16-22

AGONY!

Because J__s__s
w__ __ld b__
cr__c__f__ __d

a little while later...

JOY!

Because th__y
w__ __ld s__ __
H__m __g__ __n

Jesus would be raised back to life to beat sin and death for ever! And look at verse 22 — nothing will be able to take away Christians' joy!

AGONY!
Life can be a real pain sometimes, with hassle after hassle...

JOY!
Jesus has died and risen again for us! No one can take that joy away!

Pray!

Ask God to help you cope with any hurt in your life.
Ask Him to give you the great joy of knowing Jesus.

Just name it...

Jesus is still telling His disciples about what life will be like for them after He leaves them.

Fantastic Fact:
God loves to answer prayer!

It's totally true. Look at Jesus' amazing promise as you read...

John 16 v 23-28

What is Jesus' great promise to His followers (v23)? Find it by going back 1 letter (B=A, C=B etc).

__ __   __ __ __ __ __ __
N Z   G B U I F S

__ __ __ __
X J M M

__ __ __ __   __ __ __
H J W F   Z P V

__ __ __ __ __ __ __
X I B U F W F S

__ __ __   __ __ __   __ __
Z P V   B T L   J O

__ __   __ __ __ __
N Z   O B N F

WEIRD WORDS

Figuratively
Using picture stories, sometimes hard to understand

I can ask for whatever I want if I mention Jesus' name!

Right, I'd like loads of money, good grades, a nice boyfriend...

That's not what Jesus means!

Praying in Jesus' name means...

• Praying for things that are in line with all that Jesus stands for. Good, godly stuff. Not selfish prayers!

• Praying for things that will bring glory to Jesus. Like your friends and family becoming Christians.

• Trusting that God will answer your prayers, because Jesus has made it possible.

Pray!

Talk to God right now, using the three pointers in the box above. Try to put Jesus first (not yourself) in your prayers.

**John
16 v 29-33**

The disciples had been with Jesus for three years.

Yet they still hadn't realised that Jesus was God's Son!

But everything is about to become clear...

Keep the peace

Read John 16 v 29-32

At last! The disciples realised that Jesus was sent into the world by God. Yet Jesus told them that they would soon run away from Him when trouble arrived (v32).

A lot of what Jesus has told His disciples in the last three chapters can be summed up in three sentences. They're true for all Christians...

Find them in verse 33

1. In Jesus we have

p_____

2. In the world we'll have

tr_____

1. In Jesus we have PEACE

J_____

L_____

F_____

F_____

C_____

2. In the world we have TROUBLE

H_____

S_____

P_____

D_____

P_____

Sentence 3 tells us why Christians have peace with Jesus.

3. I have

_____

the world (v33)

Jesus died and was raised back to life to beat sin and the devil once and for all.

WEIRD WORDS

Figures of speech
Picture language

Overcome
Defeated

TROFMOC   YOJ

NOITUCESREP   NIAP

SSENEVIGROF   DERTAH

YTLUCIFFID   WORROS

EVOL   PIHSDNEIRF

Now put these 10 backwards words into the right lists of what Christians experience.

Pray!

If you're a Christian, thank Jesus that He has overcome sin and defeated death! Thank Him that one day we'll know real peace when we go to live with Him!

**John
17 v 1-5**

Target practice

Read John 17 v 1-5

*Throughout His life, Jesus had an important aim. Find it by taking every second letter, starting with the **top T**.*

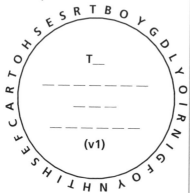

T__
__ __ __ __ __
__ __ __
__ __ __ __ __ __
(v1)

How's your aim?

*What do you **AIM** to do today or tomorrow?*

_____
_____
_____
_____
_____
_____
_____
_____

That means to show people how awesome God is. And Jesus always hit His target!

Think!

Do you have the same aim as Jesus? Do you always/sometimes/never hit the target?

Jesus will complete His work on earth (v4). So what's His aim now?

T__ GL__R__FY
H__S F__TH__R

Sorry, trick question! It's still the same! *How would Jesus glorify His Father? Take every second letter from the wheel, starting with the **top B**.*

BY _____
_____

Wow!

God sent His Son Jesus to save people. By dying on the cross for their sins, Jesus would make it possible for people to have their sins forgiven by God. They'd get to spend eternal life with God (v3)!

Pray!

Read verse 3 again. Eternal life will be great! Believers will really get to know God the Father and Jesus! If you've been saved by Jesus, you've got loads to thank Him for...

Not sure if you're a Christian? For the free e-booklet *How do I know I'm a Christian?* email discover@thegoodbook.co.uk or check out www.thegoodbook.co.uk/contact-us to find our UK mailing address.

**John
17 v 6-10**

Jesus prays for...

Pray!

Take time out right NOW to thank God loads for those people who pray for you.

Brainstorming time!

Who PRAYS for you?

_____

_____

_____

_____

_____

You might have loads of people who do, or maybe just one.

(If it's not many, ask Christian friends or family to pray for you!)

But even if you know of no one who prays for you... **Jesus is praying for you!**

Read John 17 v 6-10

Jesus was praying for the men who had spent the last three years with Him.

But check out Romans 8 v 34

Jesus prays (intercedes) for all of His followers! Christians actually belong to Jesus and He prays for them! Doesn't that make you feel excited and special?

*Find out what else Jesus says about the people He prays for. Scrub out **every third letter** in the boxes to read the answers.*

**THRE FNATPHESR GNAVLE
TQHEPM TRO HTIM (v6, 9)**

T_____

_____

They belong to the Father too! And they always will do, because Jesus has saved them. They are safe with God for ever!

**THXEY VACLCENPTSED
ZGOLD'S OWOERDNS (v8)**

T_____

_____

Jesus means His disciples especially. But everyone who belongs to Jesus believes His words. They know that Jesus is the one God sent to rescue them from their sins.

**THBEY RGLVORAIFTY
JLESPUS (v10)**

T_____

_____

That sounds impossible!

But it's not, because it brings glory to Jesus when someone becomes a Christian and begins to live for Him.

Great, eh?

Wow!

Are you one of the people Jesus calls "mine"? If you are, (especially when you feel lonely) remember that JESUS IS PRAYING FOR YOU!!

Protect and serve

John
17 v 11-15

What are you
scared of?

What really
gives you the
goosebumps?

Tick some of the
options and add
your own.

spiders ☐
great heights ☐
sloppy kisses from gran ☐
deep water ☐
snakes ☐
getting teased ☐
_____ ☐
_____ ☐

The disciples were in a scary situation. Jesus was going home to His Father in heaven, leaving the disciples in the world where they were hated for loving Jesus. How would they survive in a world that hated them?!

Read John 17 v 11-12

Jesus prayed for them!

What did He pray for them?

Find out by thinking backwards...

**Protect them by the power of
your name (v11)**

Pr_____
_____
_____
_____

Jesus had protected the disciples while He was with them. Only Judas (*"the one doomed to destruction"*) had turned away from God.

But now that Jesus was leaving them, He asked His Father to keep them safe from sin.

Read verses 13-15

**Protect them from
the evil one (v15)**

Pr_____
_____

Jesus didn't ask His Father to take them out of the world. He asked God to protect them while they stayed in the world serving God.

WEIRD WORDS

Full measure
All of it!

Wow!

Christians often have a tough time serving God. But they have God's protection! He keeps them safe from turning away from Him. That's as safe as you could possibly be!

88

**John
17 v 16-19**

Have you got a posh suit or a really nice dress that you ONLY wear on special occasions, like weddings?

It's kept nice and clean, locked away in the wardrobe and comes out maybe once a year.

WEIRD WORDS

Sanctify
Set apart for God to use

Sancti-what???

You wouldn't even dream of playing sport in it, would you?

It doesn't belong in a field, getting covered in mud.

It's set apart for a special use.

Wow!

Christians should be different from everyone else, because they don't belong to the world. Because they are **set apart for God's use.**

That's what Jesus prayed for His disciples.

Read John 17 v 16-19

**Jesus asked His Father to
s__nct__fy His disciples.**

That means He asked God to use them to serve Him.

What does that mean for Christians today?

**1. They are s__nt __nt__
th__ w__rld (v18)**

Christians are Jesus' missionaries to the world. They show the truth about Jesus by being set apart — an example to everyone. Jesus prays that His followers will be different from the world, just as He was.

**2. They live by G__d's
w__rd (v17)**

Christians live by what the Bible says. They obey God. The way Christians live should be an example to people.

**3. They are changed by
J__s__s' death (v19)**

We can't manage it by ourselves. But Jesus has the power. Christians can be set apart for God because Jesus set Himself apart for them when He died on the cross.

Think!

On paper, write how you can be different for Jesus this week...
a) at home
b) at school
Then ask God to help you!

All for one

**John
17 v 20-23**

Today's fantastic fact...

Did you know that every single Christian is joined to every other Christian, even though they don't know each other?

Sounds weird but it's true.

Find out how by joining up the people below in the right order to reveal part of **Galatians 3 v 28**.

 YOU

 JESUS

 ARE

 IN

 ONE

 ALL

CHRIST

You _____

_____

_____

_____

Christians are all joined to each other by Jesus!

Read John 17 v 20-23

Jesus prays that they will be joined in the way they...

• live like Jesus

• live for Jesus.

Then what will happen?

The world will believe that Jesus was sent by God (verses 21 and 23).

Think!

If you're a Christian, can your friends see you're different by...

a) the way you live for Jesus?

b) the way you get along with other Christians?

Action!

How can you be more like Jesus this week?

_____

_____

_____

And how can you get along better with other Christians?

_____

_____

_____

Pray!

Ask God to help you do the stuff you've written down.

**John
17 v 24-26**

Pray time

This is our last look at John's story of Jesus (until the next issue of Discover).

It's still Jesus' last evening with His disciples.

He's praying to His Father about them.

WEIRD WORDS

Glory
Jesus in all His amazing perfection

Righteous
Perfect

What would you want Jesus to pray for you? Choose one of the options or add your own idea.

> to solve all your problems

> to make you rich and famous!

> to forgive all your sins

>

See if your answer was close to what Jesus prayed for His disciples.

Read John 17 v 24 *and work it out by ignoring the Zs and Xs.*

ZZTOXBEZXWIXZXTHX
ZXZZMXEZWXZXHXEXX
XZXRXZEZIXAZXMZXXZ

To_____

_____

_____

It's the best thing anyone could ever have! Jesus prayed for His followers to be with Him. That means living with Him for ever. Now that's amazing.

Read verses 25-26
What else did Jesus pray (v26)?

ZMAXYTHZXELOXZVEZ
YOXUHAZZVEFOXZR
XMEBEXZINTZHEMXX

May_____

_____

_____

Wow!
Jesus prayed that they'd show God's love by loving Jesus and loving others.

And that Jesus would always be with His followers (v26)!

Pray!

If you're one of Jesus' followers...
a) thank God that you'll live with Jesus for ever
b) thank Him that Jesus will always be with you
c) ask God to help you show His love to others

True

Sarah Bradley

Being a Christian isn't about life becoming boring. It's about us living the way God planned and intended right from the start. Discover how to be true to yourself, your God and your relationships—with your friends, parents, church, boys—and loads more as well!

thegoodbook.co.uk/true
thegoodbook.com/true

BIBLE READING NOTES
FOR EVERY AGE AND STAGE

Adults

Explore
Various contributors

14 years plus

Engage
Martin Cole

11-13s

Discover
Martin Cole

Families

Table Talk
Alison Mitchell

7-10s

XTB (Explore the Bible)
Alison Mitchell

thegoodbook.co.uk/daily-bible-reading
thegoodbook.com/daily-devotional-reading

DISCOVER
COLLECTION

ISSUE 8

DISCOVER ISSUE 8

The Israelites learn to count on God in Numbers. Jesus pays the ultimate price for his friends in John. And prepare to have your mind blown by the good news in Romans.

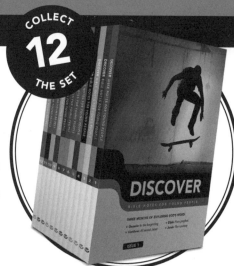

COLLECT 12 THE SET

COLLECT ALL 12 ISSUES TO COMPLETE THE DISCOVER COLLECTION

Don't forget to order the next issue of Discover. Or even better, grab a one-year subscription to make sure Discover lands in your hands as soon as it's out. Packed full of puzzles, prayers and pondering points.

thegoodbook.co.uk thegoodbook.com

thegoodbook COMPANY